The Tudors

PASSION, POWER AND POLITICS

The Tudors

PASSION, POWER AND POLITICS

EDITED BY CHARLOTTE BOLLAND

NATIONAL PORTRAIT GALLERY, LONDON

CONTENTS

6 Foreword

9 **Introduction:**
The Tudors by Charlotte Bolland

19 **A New Dynasty**
28 Insights into John Blanke's Image
from The John Blanke Project
by Michael I. Ohajuru

33 **The King's Court**
48 Walter Hungerford and the 1533
Buggery Act
by Kate O'Donoghue

53 **The Reformation in England**
62 Reginald Pole, Catholic Reform
and Religious Reconciliation
by Frederick E. Smith

67 **Queenship**
78 'We Princes Who Be Women':
Catherine de' Medici in France
by Susan Doran

83 **Holding the Throne**
94 Anthony Babington and the
Memorialisation of a Conspiracy
by Charlotte Bolland

99 **Piracy, Privateering and Trade**
108 Diego, Drake and Piracy in Panama
by Cassander L. Smith

113 **The Spanish and English Armadas**
120 'Follow Me Upon Your Honour!':
María Pita and the Siege of A
Coruña
by Monserrat Pis Marcos

125 **Empire**
138 Fighting for Survival: Gráinne O Malley
by Gillian Kenny

141 **Translation**
153 The Literary Legacy of Mary
Sidney, Countess of Pembroke
by Catharine MacLeod

156 Timeline
160 Further Reading
164 Acknowledgements
167 Picture Credits

FOREWORD

The Tudors are some of the most famous figures in English history. They have become characters within our collective imagination, performing on stage, screen and on the page for nearly five hundred years. Portraits present some of their most defining images, and the National Portrait Gallery is fortunate to hold a significant collection of these iconic works. From the power embodied in Holbein's magisterial full-length portrait of Henry VIII, to the intimacy of portrait miniatures and the extraordinary iconography created for England's second queen regnant, Elizabeth I, the stories that these portraits tell are rich and varied.

As the Gallery undergoes a major transformation, we are returning to these stories anew. My sincere thanks go to Chris Stephens, Director of the Holburne Museum, and to Laura Pye, Director of National Museums Liverpool, and Sandra Penketh, Executive Director of Galleries and Collections Management at National Museums Liverpool, for working together with the National Portrait Gallery to develop two Tudor exhibitions based on our Collection during our construction project. By working in partnership, we are able to bring new perspectives to bear on these familiar figures and to share our Collection more widely. Despite the unique challenges faced throughout 2020 and 2021, the exhibitions and accompanying publication have grown from the creative collaboration and research of the co-curators, Charlotte Bolland at the National Portrait Gallery, Monserrat Pis Marcos at the Holburne Museum, and Kate O'Donoghue at National Museums Liverpool. I am particularly delighted by the way in which this partnership, and the wide-ranging approach taken by this book through the voices of the additional contributors, has brought to the foreground some less-known, but fascinating Tudor figures. Key examples include John Blanke, trumpeter at the courts of Henry VII and Henry VIII, María Pita, defender of the town of A Coruña against the English Armada, and the poet and translator Mary Sidney, Countess of Pembroke. A thematic and international approach also offers the opportunity to tell different stories with the Collection within this book, including the challenge facing Mary I as she looked to redefine queenship in the sixteenth century, and the role of translation in shaping Tudor culture and the English language.

As is evident from the themes explored within this book, the protagonists of the portraits held by the National Portrait Gallery lived through a period of extraordinary change. In many cases, the repercussions of their actions have echoed through the centuries and created an impact that has been felt far beyond the British Isles, whether in law, language or religion. The horizons of the world in which the Tudors operated expanded rapidly over the course of the sixteenth century and it often seems as if the Tudors can be found at the beginning of many of England's global stories, instigating the country's imperial ambitions and demonstrating the means by which they would be realised, through trade, conflict and colonisation, resulting in lasting impact globally. It is therefore only fitting that, following the exhibitions in Bath and Liverpool, the Collection works will return to their place at the beginning of the chronology of the National Portrait Gallery's new displays, bringing with them the fresh perspectives revealed through this creative partnership.

Nicholas Cullinan
Director, National Portrait Gallery

WHEN YOV SEE ME,

You know me.

Or the famous Chronicle Historie of king

Henrie the Eight, with the birth and vertuous life
of EDVVARD Prince of Wales.

*As it was playd by the high and mightie Prince of Wales
his servants.*

By SAMVELL ROVVLY, servant
to the Prince.

AT LONDON,
¶ Printed for *Nathaniell Butter*, and are to be sold at his shop in Paules
Church-yard neare S. *Austines* gate. 1613.

The Tudors

Charlotte Bolland

> What is our life? A play of passion
> *On the Life of Man*, Sir Walter Ralegh

The Tudors are a cultural phenomenon. For over four hundred years since the death of Elizabeth I, the lives of the Tudor monarchs and their subjects have provided rich source material for historians, writers and artists. The period is filled with memorable characters: the six-times married king, the virgin queen, the ideal courtier, the spymaster, the explorer, the poet, the martyr. The stories of the central cast and their close social and familial networks can be followed down the generations, offering an ideal structure for the exploration of various themes within a long-running narrative. At the same time, the Tudor dynasty presided over a period of seismic change in England and Wales, which fundamentally altered the structure of society and re-shaped the country's relationship with the wider world. These two factors have encouraged subsequent generations to repeatedly return to re-examine and re-tell the stories of the Tudor period: the break with the Catholic Church in Rome and establishment of the Church of England; conflict with Spain, France and Scotland; the impact of migration triggered by religious persecution; the exploration and piracy that enabled imperial expansion and laid the foundations for trading companies that would bring unimagined wealth to the country; and the extraordinary development of

When You See Me You Know Me (title page)
Samuel Rowley, 1613
British Library C.34.e.2

the English language through poetry, drama and translation. All of these threads have been woven together over the centuries, building a cumulative storytelling power and securing the Tudors' prominence in the popular imagination.

This position has been enhanced through portraiture. Theirs is the first English royal dynasty, court and society whose faces we can encounter on the walls of galleries, in historic houses and reproduced in the books that tell their stories, through both fact and fiction. That the lives of some of the most famous Tudors have proved so engaging is in part due to the fact that it is possible to satisfy our basic human curiosity as to what they looked like. This has been recognised since the very first generation of Tudor storytellers. The first chronicles of Henry VIII and Elizabeth I's reigns to be performed on stage were titled respectively *When You See Me You Know Me* (1605) and *If You Know Not Me You Know No Bodie* (1605); John Foxe used images to powerful effect to establish the narrative of the English Reformation in his *Actes and Monuments* (1563); while Shakespeare's friends and associates ensured that his image accompanied the posthumous publication of his plays in the *First Folio* (1623).

Nonetheless, we have only a partial picture, for the majority of Tudor portraits that survive today present an elite social identity. Over the course of the sixteenth century, portraiture moved beyond being the exclusive preserve of the royal family and aristocracy in London to be commissioned by professionals and gentry families across the country. However, while the market for portraiture diversified, it was only the aristocracy and those with connections to longstanding institutions, such as the universities and livery companies, whose portraits were likely to be maintained, and the sitter's identity preserved, down the centuries. This poses a challenge. As consideration of who and how people contributed to Tudor life and culture expands beyond the people who ran the apparatus of the church and state, and the people who have been granted the spotlight by previous generations, the champions of other stories are not always able to rely on the power of portraiture to fire the historical imagination.

One unusual portrait in the collection of the National Portrait Gallery gives a sense of the scale of what is missing from our visual record of society, and perhaps an approach by which portraiture might be used to broaden the lens when considering Tudor lives. Described in the early seventeenth century as a 'story picture', the painting is both a presentation of Sir Henry Unton's likeness and a portrait of his life. Its beginning, in around 1558 in Ascott-under-Wychwood in Oxfordshire, is shown in the lower-right corner, with the infant Unton in the arms of his mother, Anne Seymour. Its end, brought about by fever during a siege of Spanish forces at La Fère attended by the doctor to the king of France, is shown at the centre, alongside the skeletal figure of Death, which hovers over Unton's shoulder in the central portrait. In between, Unton is shown in many roles: the scholar at Oxford University, the traveller in Padua and Venice, the soldier in the Low Countries, the ambassador in France and at his desk, and as the man of culture who studied, played music and hosted banquets and performances at his home. In composing each scene, the artist also provided a glimpse of the people Unton encountered: the nurse at his birth and the doctors at his death, the musicians and performers at his house, the squires and foot soldiers on the battlefield, the officers of arms in his funeral procession and the poor of Faringdon among the mourners. Unton's portrait can therefore provide a key when considering the more conventional portraits of some of the most famous Tudor figures, encouraging the viewer to bring to mind the stories of those with whom the sitters shared the stage. Some of these stories are contained within this book: people such as Walter Hungerford, the man executed alongside Thomas Cromwell; Diego, who escaped enslavement in Panama and joined Francis Drake's crew; and Gráinne O Malley, the clan chief grudgingly acknowledged by Sir Henry Sidney as the most feared sea captain in Ireland.

The portrait of Sir Henry Unton also offers a vision of Tudor life beyond the frame, for, while the painting is extraordinary, in many ways Unton's life was not. Several of the biographies of the people included in this book could be

Sir Henry Unton (c.1557–96)
Richard Scarlett, c.1596–1606
Oil on panel, 740 x 1632mm
NPG 710

An Englishman in **The Fyrst Boke of the
Introduction of Knowledge (A.iii, verso)**
Andrew Boorde, *c.*1547
London: Published for the Early English Text
Society, by N.T. Trübner & Co, 1870
The University of Leeds Library

This image became an emblem for the absurdity of
English taste. It was accompanied by a description:

> I am an English man, and naked I stand here
> Musing in my mind, what raiment I shall wear
> For now I will wear this, and now I will wear that
> Now I will wear I cannot tell what
> All new fashions be pleasant to me.

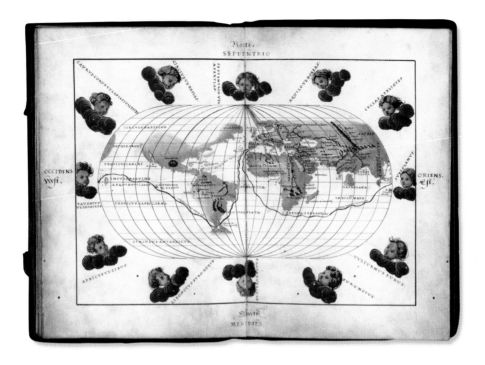

Atlas (ff.13v–14r)
Battista Agnese, *c*.1543
Lambeth Palace Library MS 463

This atlas was probably presented to Henry VIII by
the Venetian state as a gift for the young Prince
Edward. Edward was certainly interested in maps;
in 1549, he acquired Sebastian Cabot's new world
map showing the north-west passage and ordered
that it be hung at Whitehall Palace.

superimposed over at least elements of the composition, ranging from Cardinal Pole writing on Henry VIII's supremacy from Italy, to Anthony Babington plotting in Paris. As in the portrait, the Channel was simply a dividing line bisecting the scenes of many Tudor lives, regularly crossed by ambassadors, merchants, soldiers, sailors and scholars. Similarly, the prominence given to Unton's cultural life within the painting serves as a visual reminder of the way in which court culture was not only performed through the grand spectacle of royal events, but also permeated the more intimate spaces of the home, such as the intellectual circle led by Mary Sidney, Countess of Pembroke, from Penshurst. Finally, with its focus on Unton's death, the painting is a fitting reminder that, for all the confidence and self-assurance conveyed through their portraits, many of the most prominent Tudor figures died far from home: on the scaffold, at sea, on the battlefield, or put to death for their religious faith.

By the time that Unton's portrait was painted, England had transformed itself from a peripheral European power to a state that proclaimed its identity as an empire, subservient to no higher authority than the monarch. As it lost its territorial foothold in France, it opened up to a range of other cultures, attracting skilled artists, craftsmen and scholars from across Europe, and prizing novelty, ingenuity and the material value of objects in projecting the magnificence of the monarch and the country. The breadth and eclecticism of English taste was easy to ridicule, as in William Harrison's description of English clothing in his *Description of England* (1577), in which he wrote that 'such is our mutability ... that, except it were a dog in a doublet, you shall not see any so disguised as are my countrymen of England'. Nonetheless, unfettered ambition and belief in *auxilio divino* ('divine aid') saw the English looking far beyond European fashions and ideas to opportunities for trade and colonisation in the Americas and the East Indies. Thus, in 1517, when Francesco Chieregato witnessed the jousts undertaken to entertain the Spanish ambassadors, he was able to report to Isabella d'Este, who led arguably the most cultured court in Europe, that 'the wealth and civilisation of the world are here; and those who call the English barbarians appear to me to render themselves such'. The choice of the word 'barbarian' is indicative of Italian impressions of England's otherness in the early sixteenth century, a small island realm separate from mainland Europe. By the end of the century, it would be the people encountered across the Atlantic and Pacific Oceans who would commonly be termed 'barbarians'. For some, these encounters prompted self-examination. The French philosopher Michel de Montaigne noted that, given the savagery with which many people had been burned alive across Europe in the name of religion, the term 'barbarian' could no longer be so casually applied to others 'in respect of us that exceed them in all kinds of barbarism'. As with so many other ideas and innovations in the sixteenth century, Montaigne's essay 'On Cannibals' was refashioned on its arrival in England; it was translated by the Anglo-Italian John Florio and reimagined within William Shakespeare's description of a utopian society in *The Tempest*.

One of Shakespeare's most evocative descriptions provides the framework with which to approach this book. It is a selection of the stories of the men and women of Tudor England in nine acts, with some, such as Walter Ralegh, playing many parts: soldier, poet, favourite, explorer, coloniser, historian and traitor. Given his approach to the construction of Sir Henry Unton's portrait, it is tempting to imagine that the artist, the herald Richard Scarlett, might have been similarly inspired, strolling across the Thames from his house in St Botolph-without-Aldersgate north of St Paul's Cathedral to see Shakespeare's new play being performed at the recently constructed Globe Theatre:

> All the world's a stage,
> And all the men and women merely players;
> They have their exits and their entrances;
> And one man in his time plays many parts
> > *As You Like It*, William Shakespeare

Anno 1505 20 octobre ymago henricus vij tzaurigz rege illustrissimi
ordinata p hermanu zinck Lo rege ... usorum ·

A New Dynasty

On 12 February 1511, King Henry VIII of England rode through the streets of London and Westminster as his queen's champion. He was playing the part of the knight *Coeur Loyal* ('Loyal Heart'), in a two-day tournament to celebrate the birth of his son on 1 January. Only 19 years old, Henry had been king for a little under two years and was performing for his wife, Queen Katherine of Aragon, in a language of courtly chivalry that was modelled on the cultured magnificence of the Burgundian court across the Channel. The performance was ephemeral, with an elaborate forest constructed by the Office of Revels, temporary viewing platforms for the joust, and lavish golden tents in which the challengers could prepare. Heraldic devices covered every surface, with the green and white of the Tudor household decorated with red Lancastrian roses and the golden portcullis of the Beaufort family proclaiming Henry's royal lineage.

All would be swept away in the wake of the victorious champions, even the gold letters stitched to the king's clothing that fell to the floor as a demonstration of his limitless wealth and munificence. However, an image of the spectacle remains. Henry wished to remember his performance and commissioned an extraordinary record of the event from his heralds, a painted depiction of each of the stages of the tournament that covers nearly sixty feet of vellum. In the

King Henry VII (1457–1509)
Unidentified artist, 1505
Oil on panel, 425 × 305mm
NPG 416

This portrait was commissioned by the Holy Roman Emperor Maximilian I, when negotiations were underway for the recently widowed Henry VII to marry Maximilian's daughter, Margaret of Savoy.

Westminster Tournament Roll, Henry is immortalised as the star of the courtly stage, with a cast of knights, heralds, musicians and virtuous women in support.

It was no wonder that the young Henry VIII wished to document the extravagant enactment of his chivalric prowess – it was the culmination of an unlikely journey to power. He was the second son of Henry VII and the second husband of Katherine of Aragon; the death of his elder brother Arthur in 1503 brought him both the crown and – following special dispensation from the pope – his Spanish queen. His hold on the throne, and the legitimacy of Tudor rule, was also beginning to feel secure through the ruthless elimination of domestic rivals. Henry's grandparents on his father's side, Edmund Tudor, Earl of Richmond, and Lady Margaret Beaufort, had had blood ties to the royal family, but his descent from the half-brother of Henry VI and great-granddaughter of Edward III had not conferred an automatic right to the crown on Henry's father. It was only the bloodshed of the Wars of the Roses that left the Welsh-born Henry Tudor as the primary claimant to the English throne from the House

The Westminster Tournament Roll
(Membranes 25–6)
Unidentified artists, 1511
Painted vellum, 60 feet long and 14¾ inches wide
(whole roll)
College of Arms

This section of the roll shows Henry VIII jousting
before Katherine of Aragon and the wider court,
shattering his lance on his opponent's helmet on
the other side of the barrier.

of Lancaster. This in itself was not enough, and Henry Tudor had claimed
the throne by conquest from Richard III at the Battle of Bosworth in 1485. His
subsequent marriage to Elizabeth of York, the daughter and sister of the Yorkist
kings Edward IV and Edward V, allowed for the presentation of the narrative
that in their union the Wars of the Roses had come to an end, and that in their
children, and particularly in Henry VIII as king, 'the rose both red and white doth
grow'. However, Henry VIII remained aware that without an heir, there was space
for disaffected members of the aristocracy to dredge up rival claimants from the
past – a son gave him, and his dynasty, security.

It was therefore Henry's queen, Katherine, who was at the heart of the
celebrations in 1511. The daughter of the powerful joint rulers of Spain, Ferdinand
of Aragon and Isabella of Castile, it was she who elevated her husband's status
on the European stage. She brought a dowry of 200,000 ducats when she first
married Henry's brother Prince Arthur, and a personal household of scholars,
officials from the Spanish court, and musicians, among them, most likely, the

trumpeter John Blanke. Katherine could also give her children a strengthened Lancastrian claim to the English throne, as she herself was a descendant of Edward III of England through Philippa of Lancaster, who had married the king of Portugal in 1387.

Henry VII had been well aware of the importance of integrating his fledgling dynasty into the networks of European monarchies through marriage. He not only succeeded in securing a Spanish match, but also one with England's closest rival, Scotland, through the marriage of his daughter Margaret to James IV; Henry himself looked to marry into the Hapsburg dynasty after the death of Elizabeth of York, sending his portrait in 1505 to the widowed Margaret of Savoy, daughter of the Holy Roman Emperor Maximilian. In this strategy, Henry VII was following the model set by his mother, who had planned his marriage to Elizabeth of York while he was in exile in Brittany. Astute marriages had served the Tudors well.

However, it would prove to be the breakdown of Henry VIII and Katherine of Aragon's marriage that would have the most impact on the country over which they ruled, and which would set the Tudor dynasty on a new course. Only days after the celebrations at Westminster, Henry and Katherine's infant son died suddenly; they would suffer the loss of two more sons before the birth of their daughter Mary in 1516. Ultimately, Henry would repudiate his marriage of

Elizabeth of York (1466–1503)
After Maynard Wewyck, late sixteenth century, based on a work of c.1500
Oil on panel, 565 x 416mm
NPG 311

This likeness of Elizabeth of York derives from a group of portraits that Henry VII commissioned of the new Tudor royal family, which were exchanged with the rulers of Spain and Scotland during marriage negotiations.

ELIZABETHA · VXOR
HENRICI · VII ·

more than twenty years, breaking with the Catholic Church and reshaping the fabric of society in a manner that would have been inconceivable to the young man jousting in 1511. On that occasion, he was only recently returned from a pilgrimage to the Marian shrine at Walsingham Priory in Norfolk, one of the most important Catholic sites in Europe, to give thanks for the birth of his son. Twenty-seven years later, Henry's commissioners would arrive to dismantle the shrine and destroy the priory as part of the extraordinary redistribution of wealth from the church to the crown through the dissolution of the monasteries. By this point, the limitations of Henry's chivalry had also been brutally exposed. Not only had Katherine been cast aside, forced to endure the public performance of Henry's desire for one of her ladies-in-waiting, Anne Boleyn, as he jousted in the character of a tortured lover wearing the motto 'Declare I dare not', but Anne herself had been executed at the order of the man who had once styled himself 'Sir Loyal Heart'.

Overleaf:

Lady Margaret Beaufort (1443–1509)
After Pietro Torrigiano, 1875, based on a work of c.1514
Electrotype, 889mm high
NPG 356

Lady Margaret's role in establishing the Tudor dynasty is commemorated in the placement of her tomb in the south aisle of Henry VII's chapel in Westminster Abbey. The tomb was commissioned by Henry VIII from the Florentine sculptor Pietro Torrigiano, and includes a Latin inscription composed by the Dutch humanist Desiderius Erasmus.

King Henry VIII (1491–1547)
Unidentified artist, c.1520
Oil on panel, 508 x 381mm
NPG 4690

Katherine of Aragon (1485–1536)
Unidentified artist, c.1520
Oil on panel, 520 x 420mm
NPG L246

Many versions of these portraits of Henry VIII and Katherine of Aragon were produced during the course of their marriage. The paintings are of a similar scale and share a damask background, which suggests that they could have been displayed as a pair. Poignantly, an inventory taken after Katherine's death records that she had kept paired images of herself and Henry.

Insights into John Blanke's Image from The John Blanke Project

Michael I. Ohajuru

John Blanke has become the poster boy for the Black presence in Tudor England. He alone is seen on the covers of books and magazines, his visual presence helping us rewrite and reimagine British history. Today, to the vocal frustration of some, historians are rewriting parts of that history, embracing less well-known figures such as John Blanke. They are shedding light on ordinary men and women, the poor, those with disabilities, Black folk – those seen as marginal in the conventional view of a history presented around the exploits of the great white men of the day such as Henry VIII, Thomas More, Thomas Cromwell and others. *The John Blanke Project* is a part of that rewriting, an art and archive project that celebrates the Black trumpeter to the Tudor court reimagined by artists and historians from those two distinctive images in the Westminster Tournament Roll and his brief presence in the written Tudor court accounts found in The National Archives.

The Project has offered new insight into John Blanke's image, what it meant when first produced and what that image means today. Some were mundane yet thought-provoking, such as when a primary school student told me that they 'imagined John Blanke as a strong man because he could ride a horse and play the trumpet at the same time'. The skill and strength required to do both while keeping time and pace with the other trumpeters and the procession were new considerations. Other perspectives gained from the project were not so prosaic, but were equally intriguing: how special it was to have a recognisable image of a non-noble Tudor sitter, the significance of depicting his difference both in skin colour and dress, the meaning behind his name, and the implications of our desire to treat him as exceptional.

A Remarkable Portrait

Portraits of recognisable, named non-noble sitters such as John Blanke were very rare in the early Tudor period. His double representation on the Westminster Tournament Roll is extraordinary, as portraiture was a new form of visual representation at the time reserved for those of high status and powerful elites such as Henry VIII and close members of his court. The image is a thumbnail sketch, a caricature, yet with sufficient detail to give John Blanke a strong visual presence, his dark brown skin tone and distinctive headgear setting him apart from the white, bare-headed trumpeters in the troop. Certainly, the scribe did not produce lifelike portrait sketches as Holbein was to do a few years later of Henry and his court. Nevertheless, he created an image with sufficient detail for us to put a name to the figure from court records, making it a truly remarkable portrait for the time.

Accepting Difference

It is not just John Blanke's dark brown skin tone that makes him different from his fellow white trumpeters. They are all bare-headed while he alone wears headwear. The multicoloured patterned cloth of his headdress is religious and cultural, rather than a convention or fashion statement, perhaps indicating he had once been Muslim, or at least had been raised in a Muslim cultural context. It contrasts sharply with the headwear of processing Gentlemen of the Court and Henry VIII, for they all wear flat caps of different colours and materials festooned with feathers and, in Henry's case, jewels. The Roll allows us to glimpse an occasion when the Tudor court permitted a member of the royal households to wear a marker of Islamic religious faith and cultural difference that contravened the normal insistence on the homogeneity of livery in quite an extraordinary fashion, making John Blanke even more distinctive.

John Blanke's Namesakes

His name is not as special as his image. It is perhaps an attempt to highlight the difference in John Blanke's skin colour when compared to others, at a time before race was used to create that difference. John Blanke is a nickname, punning on the colour of his skin, as 'blanc' is the French for 'white'. There were other Black Africans in Europe with very similar names: in fourteenth-century Spain an enslaved 'Johan Blanc' was given as a gift by the king of Aragon to King John the Good of France; in fifteenth-century Venice one 'Zuan Bianco' was a courageous commander of infantry in the Venetian army (Shakespeare may have drawn on him indirectly in conceiving his own Black Venetian commander, Othello), and in seventeenth-century Spain 'Juan Alba' (in Latin, 'alba' means 'white') was a courageous African soldier in the play *The Valiant Black in Flanders*.

Black British History and John Blanke

The most profound insight of the project has been that, by making John Blanke an exception, he is marginalised and his existence made strange. This exceptionalism can help maintain prejudices and, in doing so, marginalise him as an anomaly. The research and writings of historians have shown there are many more Black Africans in Tudor society, some of whom we know far more about – it is only John Blanke's image which makes him exceptional when compared to other Black Tudors. John Blanke is important and he is rightly highlighted here. But only when he becomes less important and not seen as an exception will we actually begin to understand him, Britain's history, and the Black African role in that history more clearly.

***The Westminster Tournament Roll
(Membrane 28)***
Unidentified artists, 1511
Painted vellum, 60 feet long and 14¾ inches wide (whole roll)
College of Arms

First documented in the royal household in 1507, John Blanke was well established as one of the royal trumpeters by the time of the Westminster Tournament. Records show that he successfully petitioned Henry VIII to double his salary and that the king gifted him a violet gown for his own wedding.

Tribute to John Blanke
Stephen B. Whatley, 2015
Charcoal on paper, 297 x 210mm
The John Blanke Project Collection

The King's Court

One of the greatest portraits of the Tudor period is lost, destroyed in the fire that consumed Whitehall Palace on 4 January 1698. Painted on a wall as part of the lavish development of the palace, the portrait was intended to overwhelm the viewer with the majesty of the second Tudor king. Henry VIII was depicted at full-length, standing square on and staring out at his subjects. While the king was undoubtedly the main focus, the portrait celebrated the Tudor dynasty and its future: Henry's father stood behind him and on the other side of the composition stood his mother, Elizabeth of York, and Henry's third wife Jane Seymour. At the time the portrait was conceived Jane was pregnant; just as with the celebrations at Westminster twenty-five years earlier, Henry's queen was key to the performance of his power. Following the break with the Catholic Church in Rome in order to secure his divorce from Katherine of Aragon, Henry had assumed the title of Supreme Head of the Church of England. It is therefore not surprising that the potency of the portrait of the king was immediately recognised. The preparatory cartoon for the mural was soon being used to create copies of Henry's image, stamping his authority on spaces beyond the palace walls as a fitting demonstration of the way in which his temporal and spiritual power was, in the words of the French ambassador, making him 'not only a King to be obeyed, but an icon to be worshipped'.

King Henry VIII (1491–1547)
Workshop of Hans Holbein the Younger, *c*.1537
Oil on panel, 2390 x 1345mm
National Museums Liverpool,
Walker Art Gallery, No. 1350

This is one of the earliest portraits of Henry derived from the Whitehall mural; its provenance suggests that it was commissioned by a member of the Seymour family.

34

The portrait was the work of the newly appointed 'King's Painter', the German artist Hans Holbein the Younger. Holbein produced a variety of work during his time at Henry VIII's court, ranging from decorative schemes for lavish performances to entertain visiting ambassadors, to the design of jewels and metalwork. However, it is for his portraits that Holbein is perhaps most celebrated. Just as for his original clients, Holbein's meticulous approach to portraiture seems to bring us into the presence of the people who populated Henry VIII's court, not only the royal family, the aristocracy and statesmen, but also religious leaders and intellectuals, merchants trading in London, and fellow members of the royal household. The lives of these sitters reveal the opportunities for advancement offered by the court, and the danger of carving out a career under a capricious king who used the appetite for religious reform to seize more power than had been held by any other English monarch, and

Overleaf:

Sir Thomas More (1478–1535)
After Hans Holbein the Younger, early seventeenth century, based on a work of 1527
Oil on panel, 749 x 584mm
NPG 4358

Thomas More was Holbein's first patron in England. Holbein's portrait survives in the Frick Collection, New York.

King Henry VIII (1491–1547)
After Hans Holbein the Younger, probably seventeenth century, based on a work of 1536
Oil on copper, 279 x 200mm
NPG 157

A copy of the only surviving painting of Henry VIII by Holbein, a small-scale portrait now in the Thyssen-Bornemisza Museum, Madrid.

William Warham (1450?–1532)
After Hans Holbein the Younger, early seventeenth century, based on a work of 1527
Oil on panel, 822 x 663mm
NPG 2094

Holbein painted at least two versions of his portrait of Warham, one of which was kept in Lambeth Palace and now survives in the Louvre, Paris.

who demanded absolute loyalty. The dynamic between Henry and Holbein is impossible to trace, but an anecdote recounted by Holbein's first biographer, Karel van Mander, in the seventeenth century suggests that the king prized the artist's skills, informing a shocked earl who had attempted to complain about Holbein that 'I can make seven earls (if it pleased me) from seven peasants – but I could not make one Holbein, or so excellent an artist, out of seven earls'. One source that raises intriguing questions is the comparison between the preparatory cartoon for the Whitehall mural and the final painting, as preserved in copies. In the first, Henry is presented in a three-quarter view, similar to that seen in a small jewel-like portrait that may have been commissioned as a diplomatic gift; in the second, Henry confronts the viewer directly. Was this shift, which created one of the most iconic depictions of power in Western art, the vision of the artist, or the sitter?

Holbein's journey to England exemplifies the way in which artists, musicians, merchants, poets and soldiers were able to gain access to the court through social networks. Many came from other countries, and although foreigners residing in England could be ordered to leave at any time, such deportation orders often included the crucial caveat that 'all strangers in the service of the King, the Queen, my Lord Prince, or any of the King's other children ... shall remain as long as they shall be in such service'. Holbein's first contacts in England were made through the Dutch humanist Erasmus, who corresponded from Basel with Thomas More; William Warham, Archbishop of Canterbury; and John Fisher, Bishop of Rochester. The men exchanged their portraits, exploiting

Nicholas Kratzer (b.1486/7, d. after 1550)
After Hans Holbein the Younger, late sixteenth century, based on a work of 1528
Oil on panel, 819 x 648mm
NPG 5245

Kratzer is portrayed holding a pair of dividers and an unfinished polyhedral dial; the Latin inscription describes him as a Bavarian from Munich, and records that the portrait was taken from life when he was in his forty-first year. Holbein's portrait survives in the Louvre, Paris.

Holbein's lifelike style as a means of bridging the geographical distance that separated them. On arriving in London, Holbein also found work with the German merchant community operating out of the Steelyard, and developed contacts with the court. These included the king's astronomer, and tutor to Thomas More's children, Nicholas Kratzer, with whom Holbein designed a ceiling decoration of the heavens for the 1527 celebrations at Greenwich in honour of the French ambassadors.

The movement of skilled craftsmen between cities was often regulated in the sixteenth century, and Holbein was forced to return to Basel in 1528 as he had only been granted a two-year leave of absence by the city authorities. However, it was only a temporary homecoming, and whether in search of patronage or feeling discomfort at the extent of religious reforms in the city, which had resulted in acts of iconoclasm, Holbein returned to England in 1532. In that year, Thomas More resigned as Chancellor in protest at the annulment of Henry VIII's marriage to Katherine of Aragon, and the death of William Warham allowed Henry to nominate Thomas Cranmer as Archbishop of Canterbury. Holbein secured the patronage of the new powers at court, painting Thomas Cromwell's portrait in 1533 and designing gifts for Anne Boleyn to present to Henry VIII. His skill seems to have allowed him to navigate the factions and religious divisions that were poisoning the court, receiving the commission to design the

Thomas Cromwell, Earl of Essex (c.1485–1540)
After Hans Holbein the Younger, early seventeenth century, based on a work of 1532–3
Oil on panel, 781 x 691mm
NPG 1727

The letter on the table identifies Cromwell as Master of the Jewel House, one of the first posts he held before he became chief minister. Holbein's portrait survives in the Frick Collection, New York.

EARL OF ESSEX.

frontispiece for the new translation of the Bible into English in 1535 and to paint the portrait of the arch religious conservative Thomas Howard, Duke of Norfolk in 1539.

However, all were at risk in Henry's court. As Thomas More counselled a courtier in a poem: 'You often boast to me that you have the king's ear and often have fun with him ... This is like having fun with tamed lions – often it is harmless, but just as often there is fear of harm. Often he roars in rage for no known reason, and suddenly the fun becomes fatal.' Once the king's most trusted advisor, More was beheaded on 6 July 1535, two weeks after Cardinal John Fisher, after both refused to take the Oath of Supremacy recognising Henry VIII as head of the Church of England. The execution of such prominent and revered figures sent shockwaves across Europe, and Holbein's portraits of both came to serve as memorials that were copied repeatedly over the centuries. It was not only religious figures, both the 'new men' of Henry's court and the aristocracy were vulnerable. Cromwell was executed on 28 July 1540, while the duke of Norfolk was only spared execution by Henry's death on 28 January 1547. The climate of fear at court was vividly described by the French ambassador Charles de Marillac after the executions of Cromwell and Lord Hungerford. He blamed the king's greed, inconstancy and fear: 'This King, knowing how many changes he has made, and what tragedies and scandals he has created, would fain keep in favour with everybody, but does not trust a single man, expecting to see them all offended,

John Fisher (1469–1535)
After Hans Holbein the Younger, sixteenth century, based on a work of c.1532
Oil on paper, 210 x 191mm
NPG 2821

This face pattern was used to produce versions of Fisher's portrait. It survived among a rare group of patterns used in a sixteenth-century artist's studio.

**King Henry VIII (1491–1547) and
King Henry VII (1457–1509)**
Hans Holbein the Younger, c.1536–7
Ink and watercolour, 2578 x 1372mm
NPG 4027

Hans Holbein the Younger (c.1497–1543)
Unidentified artist, mid- or late sixteenth century
Gouache on vellum on playing card,
36mm (diameter)
Wallace Collection M203

and he will not cease to dip his hand in blood as long as he doubts his people.'

After Henry VIII's death, leaving a young son to rule under the guidance of a group of councillors and a country riven with religious division, the fear and uncertainty of the English court remained as factions sought to retain power. Two of the earliest surviving copies of Holbein's portrait of Henry VIII have provenance tracing back to the Seymour family. Their display of portraits demonstrated their position as relatives by marriage to the king, and by blood to the future Edward VI; however, even their security was short-lived. Jane Seymour's brothers Edward and Thomas assumed the roles of Lord Protector and High Admiral during the reign of their nephew, but, envious of his brother, Thomas sought to discredit Edward, and was ultimately executed for treason in March 1549 after trying to break into the king's apartments. Later that same year, Edward's position came under threat from John Dudley, Duke of Northumberland; Edward was executed in January 1552, with his young nephew blandly noting in his personal chronicle: 'the duke of Somerset had his head cut off upon Tower Hill between eight and nine o'clock in the morning'.

King Edward VI (1537–53)
Unidentified artist, c.1547
Oil on panel, 1556 x 813mm
NPG 5511

This portrait was produced to mark Edward VI's investiture as Prince of Wales but had to be hastily updated in January 1547 by the addition of the royal arms, to reflect his accession to the throne after the death of his father.

Walter Hungerford and the 1533 Buggery Act

Kate O'Donoghue

On 28 July 1540, Thomas Cromwell, once the highly esteemed and powerful statesman, was beheaded on Tower Hill after falling dramatically from Henry VIII's favour. His death represents one of the most famous and ruthless executions of the king's reign. Alongside him and suffering the same fate was a much lesser-known individual, Walter Hungerford. Like Cromwell, Hungerford had previously enjoyed the friendship of the king and had served as a squire to Henry in his youth. Hungerford's death was extraordinary for another reason – it was the first execution following a formal charge under the Buggery Act of 1533. This Act represents the first secular law in England which criminalised sexual activity between men. It would have devastating consequences for LGBTQ+ communities and individuals across the world for generations to come.

The 1533 Buggery Act was an important instrument in the Dissolution of the Monasteries between 1536 and 1541. The Reformation marked a radical shift in English society and prompted widespread suspicion, distrust and fear. The *Valor Ecclesiasticus*, a survey ordered by Henry in 1535, detailed the extensive wealth held by monasteries in England, Wales and some parts of Ireland. Despite the shift away from Catholicism by this time, monasteries were highly respected by the public. They were regarded as charitable and educational institutions and were held up as models of morality. As Henry himself would later phrase it in a 1543 letter to his ambassador in Scotland, 'The extirpation of monks and friars requires politic handling.' In order to establish himself as the new moral authority, Henry needed to find a way to discredit the monasteries. The most convenient and effective way to do this was to accuse them of sexual immorality.

The Buggery Act made the 'detestable and abominable vice of buggery' punishable by death. Prior to this, church courts dealt with issues of morality, but cases of same-sex activity were seldom addressed and were usually treated leniently. Crucially, the Act stated that men in religious orders were not exempt from execution, as they sometimes were for other crimes. In 1535, Cromwell arranged formal 'visitations' on England's monasteries. Officials were sent with a 'secret commission to groundly examine all the religious' in order to 'learn all their abominations'.

Monks faced intimidation and harassment in order to force confessions, resulting in the *Comperta*, or 'Disclosures', which detailed a litany of abuse and scandal. One of Cromwell's agents, Richard Layton, was particularly scathing in his reports. Layton refers to one abbot as 'the drunkenest knave living', and another cleric, a prior, as the 'monk *maximus sodomita*'. Though specific references to same-sex activity are only clear in a small number of reports, the *Comperta* gave the impression that this was widespread, with vast numbers of monks labelled 'sodomites'. 'Buggery' had a conveniently vague definition, and for the Tudors it became an umbrella term for anything perceived as a sexual deviation. It was applied to a wide variety of offences, including witchcraft and bestiality, which was considered intimacy with the devil in animal form. When the reports were read in Parliament, the response was condemnation and uproar. The campaign was swift and effective, and by 1541 the monasteries were dissolved, and their wealth transferred to Henry and his supporters.

Despite the impact and leverage of the Buggery Act, Walter Hungerford, Baron of Heytesbury, was the only person executed under the Act during Henry's reign. Bleak accounts detail Hungerford's cruel and abusive treatment of his wife, Elizabeth. Her letters describe her imprisonment at Farleigh Castle for three to four years, and her husband's attempts to starve and poison her. Elizabeth wrote pleas to Cromwell, Hungerford's patron, which went largely unanswered. Hungerford only came under scrutiny when Cromwell was arrested for treason in 1540. He was soon faced with numerous defamatory accusations, including buggery and witchcraft. Significantly, he was also charged with treason for employing a priest, William Bird, who was an outspoken critic of Henry VIII's assault on the monasteries. Hungerford was supporting Henry's enemies and, in doing so, grossly offended the king. The charge of buggery, considered his most heinous crime, was likely a partly political move intended to strengthen the case against him. It served to disgrace his name as well as that of his associate, Cromwell.

Although Mary I repealed the Buggery Act when she succeeded in 1553, it was reinstated by Elizabeth I in 1563. Scarcely implemented during Elizabeth's reign, the Act's influence resonates throughout the following centuries and into the present day. It remained in place until the Offences Against the Person Act in 1828, and buggery remained a capital offence until 1861. The Act's impact was particularly brutal in the eighteenth and nineteenth centuries, when many individuals lost their lives and hundreds more were imprisoned. Moreover, the Buggery Act found itself exported across the British Empire in various iterations, and laws criminalising same-sex activity became a common thread of British Imperial rule. As the British Empire expanded throughout the centuries, it enforced penal codes devised for its colonies, such as the Indian Penal Code of 1860.

In some jurisdictions, sexual activity between women was also specifically prohibited. In many parts of Asia and Africa, there was no clear existence of such laws before they were imposed by the British Empire. Homosexuality was only partially decriminalised in England and Wales in 1967, with the last of the laws criminalising same-sex activity repealed in the 2003 Sexual Offences Act. Many countries still have discriminatory laws in place today.

The Buggery Act gave Henry, already ruling monarch and Head of the Church of England, tremendous power. Essential in his campaign to dismantle the Catholic Church's authority in England, the Act enabled Henry to inhabit a role of moral superiority. It gave him leverage to vilify his enemies and smear those who offended him. Although some details around Hungerford's case are unclear, he represents one of many to suffer under the Act and its various successors. It remains one of Henry's most devastating and enduring legacies.

Panorama of London as seen from Southwark:
The Tower
Anthonis van der Wijngaerde, 1554
Pen and ink over indications in black chalk,
245 x 423mm
Ashmolean Museum WA1950.206.11

*Actis made in the session of this present
parliament holden uppon prorogation at
Westmynster, the .XV. daye of Januarie, in the.
XXV. yere of the reigne of our moste dradde
soueraygne lorde kynge Henry the. VIII.*
Printed by Thomas Berthelet, 1535
British Library 506.d.33

The Pope Suppressed by King Henry VIII
Unidentified artist, 1570
Woodcut, 188 x 175mm
NPG D23436

This image was created as an illustration for
the second edition of John Foxe's *Actes and
Monuments*.

The Reformation in England

Over a twenty-year period in the mid-sixteenth century, England was transformed from a Catholic country to a Protestant one. The Act of Restraints in Appeals in 1533 swept away the authority of the pope and in so doing established the legal foundation of the Reformation in England, enabling a programme of religious reform driven by the monarch as Supreme Head of the Church. When Henry VIII died in the early hours of 28 January 1547, it was with Thomas Cranmer, Archbishop of Canterbury and the architect of the new religion in England, by his bedside. Thirty years had passed since the German friar Martin Luther had written his 'Ninety-Five Theses' against corruption among the Catholic clergy, fuelling an appetite for religious reform that spread across Europe. In that time, Henry had gone from penning a critique of Luther that encouraged Pope Leo X to grant him the title 'Defender of the Faith' to repudiating the very notion of papal authority in England.

The new hierarchy is vividly depicted in a woodcut showing Henry enthroned and trampling Pope Clement VII beneath his feet. Thomas Cromwell and Thomas Cranmer pass a book to the king, presumably the English translation of the Bible that they both championed, while Bishop Fisher and Cardinal Pole attempt to aid the pope and tonsured monks look on in horror. The image was produced during Elizabeth I's reign as part of a move to consolidate the Anglican Church through the creation of a consistent narrative of religious reform. The reality of the 1530s and 1540s was very different, with Henry VIII often seeming to careen between religious reform and conservatism under the influence of different factions at court. People from both sides of the confessional divide faced death for their beliefs if perceived to be a threat to the state. The French

King Edward VI and the Pope
Unidentified artist, c.1575
Oil on panel, 622 x 908mm
NPG 4165

The anti-papal message of this painting may well have been inspired by Pope Pius V's excommunication of Elizabeth I in 1570. Henry VIII gestures from his deathbed towards his son, who sits above an open book bearing the inscription 'THE WORD OF YE LORD ENDURET FOREVER' and a portrayal of the pope cowed by the words 'IDOLATORY', 'SUPERSTITION' and 'FEIGNED HOLINESS'. It is likely that the white squares were intended to hold additional inscriptions but no trace of text remains. Edward's council sit to his left, beneath a scene of iconoclasm in which men pull down statues.

ambassador Marillac marvelled in August 1540 that the executions of Cromwell and Hungerford had been followed by both the hanging of three men as traitors for speaking in favour of the pope and the burning of three men as heretics. However, Henry remained constant to one newfound belief – the church in England was under his personal authority, and this control would pass to his son.

Assuming the throne at only 9 years old, Edward's personal impact on the course of the Reformation in England has been much debated. To some he was the new Josiah, the boy king from the Old Testament who had destroyed the altars and temples of false gods; to others a pawn, manipulated first by his uncle Edward Seymour as Lord Protector, and then by John Dudley as Lord President of the Council. Perhaps both are partly true. Raised as a Protestant and educated by humanists who were committed to evangelical reform, Edward keenly engaged with the debates that were shaping the direction of religious reform, taking notes when listening to sermons, and writing a treatise against papal supremacy and affirming his personal adherence to the doctrine of salvation by faith. At the same time, the bypassing of conciliar rule by both Seymour and Dudley centred authority in the hands of two men who were committed to advancing reform in England. Together, the king and his councillors transformed the country. Where Henry had stripped the monasteries and siphoned their wealth to the crown, Edward and his council extended religious change into the daily ritual life of the population. Candles and shrines were banned, and then images in stained-glass, wood and stone. At the same time, the language of religion was forcibly changed into English through Cranmer's *Book of Common Prayer*, creating a uniform vernacular service of worship for the first time.

These changes placed England at the forefront of wider European debates about the many possible paths that religious reform could take. As a state with a committed Protestant leadership, England offered a refuge for reformers in exile from countries across the continent. Many were invited by Cranmer to cross the Channel to a new haven. Of the men who would later be celebrated as the leading theologians of the Reformation, three spent extended periods in England during Edward's reign: the German Martin Bucer, the Italian Peter Martyr Vermigli and the Scot John Knox. Although Cranmer's ambitions to host an international church council to rival the Catholic Council of Trent – with invitations sent to Heinrich Bullinger, John Calvin and Philip Melanchthon – came to nothing, the establishment of the London Stranger Church in 1550 under the supervision of the Polish Calvinist John à Lasco created a space for émigré Protestant congregations. However, not all were welcome, and the Stranger Church also offered a means to monitor any radical evangelicals who were championing equality in society as well as in religious practice.

England had changed, but all could be undone. The reforms achieved by 1550 came at great cost, having prompted two major rebellions that challenged the extension of the state's authority: the Pilgrimage of Grace in the north of the country in 1536 and the Prayer Book Rebellion in the south-west in 1549. The reformers needed time to consolidate, but when Edward fell dangerously ill in 1553, their time ran out. Edward's eldest sister, Mary, had defiantly continued to attend Catholic Mass throughout his reign, and, as an unmarried woman, she was thought likely not only to restore Catholicism but also to invite foreign influence into the country through marriage to a foreign prince. Mapping out the future line of succession in his last months, Edward looked to his cousin, Lady Jane Grey, who had been educated by the same Cambridge-trained

Thomas Cranmer (1489–1556)
Gerlach Flicke, 1545–6
Oil on panel, 984 x 762mm
NPG 535

Offering a deliberate counter to the Catholic iconography of Holbein's portrait of William Warham, Cranmer's books in this portrait emphasise his reformed position on the theology of justification by faith.

***The Candle is Lighted, We Can Not Blow
Out (Leading Theologians of the Protestant
Reformation)***
Published by John Garrett, after 1673
Line engraving, 257 x 372mm
NPG D24005

Although many of the new Protestant doctrines
were antagonistic to each other, the key individuals
leading the debates were perceived as being
united by their desire for religious reform. In this
seventeenth-century image, a cardinal, the devil,
the pope and a monk attempt to blow out the
candle of Protestantism that sits before Martin
Luther at the centre of the table.

***A Description of Master Latimer, Preaching
Before King Edward the Sixth, in the Preaching
Place at Westminster***
Unidentified artist, mid-sixteenth century
Woodcut, 145 x 181mm
NPG D23050

The preaching place commissioned by Edward VI
for the grounds of Whitehall Palace in Westminster,
and from which the young king would listen to
sermons, is celebrated in this woodcut from Foxe's
Actes and Monuments.

evangelicals as he had been, to secure the Protestant cause in England. This was likely prompted by Jane's marriage to Lord Guildford Dudley – the son of John Dudley, Duke of Northumberland, who was effectively ruling the country in his role as Lord President of the Council. However, it was Mary who was able to rally support and return authority over the church in England to the pope in Rome once she was crowned queen in 1553.

The speed of Catholic restoration may have surprised those leading Protestants who had hoped for a simple retreat from public life at Mary's accession, but the intertwining of politics and religion meant that many could be arrested for treason and sedition before facing trial for heresy. These included the Archbishop of Canterbury Thomas Cranmer, Bishop of Worcester Hugh Latimer and Bishop of London Nicholas Ridley, each of whom was burned at the stake on Broad Street in Oxford following lengthy debates with Catholic investigators over many months. The threat of arrest and execution reversed the currents of migration from Edward's reign, with committed Protestants crossing the Channel to escape England. However, most of the population welcomed the return of Mass, and the return to churches of the treasured sculptures and sacred objects that had evaded destruction during Edward's reign. Rebellion rose in Kent, led by the Protestant Thomas Wyatt, but it gathered support for its resistance to Mary's proposed marriage to Philip II of Spain, rather than in defence of the changes that had been enacted across England in the preceding decades.

Nonetheless, England's Reformation ultimately endured, as Mary's death without an heir swung the pendulum once again in its favour. It was the Protestant hagiographers of Elizabeth I's reign who were able to set down the first histories of the reigns of Henry VIII, Edward VI and Mary I. Chief among these was John Foxe in his *Actes and Monuments*, first published in 1563 and more commonly known as 'Foxe's Book of Martyrs'. Its anti-Catholic message was enhanced through woodcut illustrations that would shape the narrative of the 'horrible and bloodye tyme' of England's first queen regnant, Mary, for centuries to come.

The Burning of the Archbyshop of Caunterbury
Doctour Thomas Cranmer
Unidentified artist, 1563 or later
Woodcut, 146 x 192mm
NPG D34254

In one of the most famous images from Foxe's *Actes and Monuments*, Thomas Cranmer places his hand into the flames to renounce his earlier recantation of his Protestant beliefs before 'Friar John', the Spanish Dominican Juan de Villagarcía, who had been brought to England by Philip II of Spain.

Reginald Pole, Catholic Reform and Religious Reconciliation

Frederick E. Smith

In the summer of 1535, the English nobleman Reginald Pole sat down in his Italian residence and composed an extended letter to Henry VIII. A cousin of the English king, Pole had been asked for his opinion on recent religious developments in his homeland, particularly the 1534 Act of Supremacy that had declared Henry VIII Supreme Head of the English Church. Pole's letter, which he grandly entitled *Pro ecclesiasticae unitatis defensione (Defence of the Unity of the Church)*, made his stance abundantly clear. By claiming power properly pertaining to the pope, Pole argued, Henry had endangered not just his own soul, but the souls of all his subjects. Pole did little to hide his outrage: 'To everyone,' he told the English king, 'you appear more cruel than any pirate, more bold than Satan himself.'

With this letter, Pole became one of the most outspoken opponents of the English Reformation. Having effectively exiled himself from his homeland, he moved to Rome where he was made a cardinal in 1536. Over the next eighteen years, he became involved in a series of plots and schemes designed to return England to papal obedience, either through persuasion or force. These included attempts to orchestrate popular resistance within England itself, as well as overtures to the Spanish Emperor Charles V, calling upon his support for an economic blockade.

Pole's efforts were all ultimately unsuccessful and did nothing to prevent the progress of the Reformation in Henrician and Edwardian England. However, they did succeed in provoking the ire of the English regime. Pole's name was repeatedly attacked in government propaganda, which denounced him as a treacherous 'papist' who 'wouldst have drowned thy country in blood'. Agents and assassins were dispatched abroad to infiltrate the cardinal's inner circle, and members of Pole's family remaining in England were executed.

With the accession of the Catholic Princess Mary to the English throne in 1553, Pole's fortunes changed dramatically. He was made papal legate to England and returned home in 1554 in order to restore the realm to papal obedience. Following the execution of Thomas Cranmer in 1556, Pole was made Archbishop of Canterbury. Under his leadership, Catholic worship was restored in the parishes and a brutal campaign against Protestantism was launched, resulting in the burning of almost 300 men and women.

This portrait of Pole – the staunch Catholic opponent of the English Reformation – is how he usually appears in histories of Tudor England. However, taking a broader, more international perspective on the English cardinal's life, a rather different picture begins to emerge. Despite his opposition to the Reformation in England, Pole was deeply interested in religious reform. Over the years he spent in Italy, he gathered a group of like-minded churchmen, theologians and intellectuals around him – a group whose members came to refer to themselves as the *spirituali*, or 'spiritual ones'. Together this group discussed works by prominent Catholic theologians, but also those written by Protestant reformers such as Martin Luther and John Calvin. Their hope was that, by taking the ideas and criticisms of Protestants seriously, cleansing the Catholic Church of corruption and reforming certain aspects of Catholic doctrine, they might heal the growing rift within Christendom.

Pole advocated this open and conciliatory approach to reform at the Council of Trent, an influential meeting of Catholic prelates first convened in 1545 in order to decide an appropriate response to the Protestant threat. Pole delivered a keynote address to the Council, imploring the delegates to keep an open mind, to 'read all books, even of adversaries', and to 'refuse to say automatically, "Luther said that, therefore it is false"'.

Pole's passionate entreaties fell on deaf ears. Although the Council did address issues such as clerical corruption and laxity, it ultimately quashed any prospect of reconciliation by declaring against several key Protestant doctrines. Pole's most powerful opponent at the Council was Gian Pietro Carafa, head of the Italian Inquisition, who regarded the *spirituali* approach to reform as nothing short of heretical. Carafa's influence within the Catholic Church grew significantly when, in 1555, he was elected Pope Paul IV. He subsequently launched a series of investigations into the *spirituali*, resulting in the imprisonment of several of Pole's former associates. At the time of his death in 1558, Pole himself had been summoned to Rome where he faced eighteen charges of heresy.

The tension between Pole, opponent of the English Reformation and persecutor of Protestants in Marian England, and Pole, passionate advocate of inter-confessional dialogue and reconciliation, has perplexed observers for hundreds of years. As one contemporary noted in the 1560s, Pole died being considered 'a Lutheran in Rome and a papist in Germany'. However, if Pole's life teaches us anything, it is the dangers of applying labels such as 'Protestant' and 'Catholic' too rigidly during this period.

REGNALDVS POLVS.
Principis e stirpe et magni cognominis hæres
Exul, amat patrios ROMÆ mutare penates   Æ

Reginald Pole (1500–58)
Magdalena de Passe, or Willem de Passe, 1620
Line engraving, 153 x 113mm
NPG D24898

The Latin caption below the image reads as
follows: 'Reginald Pole, from a princely lineage and
heir to a great name, an exile, he loves to change
his fatherland's hearths for those of Rome.'

Queenship

In 1553, Edward VI attempted to prevent his Catholic half-sister Mary from becoming England's first queen regnant. However, Edward was faced with a challenge: all the alternative candidates to succeed him were women. His solution, as he sought to preserve Protestantism in England, was for his cousin, Lady Jane Grey, to act as a governor and hold power with a council until she had a son who could assume the throne. Two of his stepmothers, Katherine of Aragon and Katherine Parr, had held just such a role to great effect during Henry VIII's absences on campaign in France. The lengths to which Edward thought the country would go to find a new king is evident in the number of female relatives whose unborn sons and grandsons he listed as his heirs in his 'Devise' for the succession. Only a hasty revision, made as it became clear that Edward would die before any of these male heirs were born, clarified that Lady Jane Grey could succeed in her own right. However, in a competition between two female claimants, the scribbled changes that Jane's supporters could use to justify her claim were no match for the power base that Mary had built up over many years. Jane was able to hold her position for a mere nine days, with Mary riding triumphantly into London less than a month after Edward's death. However, Mary was faced with the same challenge that had blinded Edward to

Lady Jane Grey (1537–54)
Unidentified artist, late sixteenth century
Oil on panel, 856 x 603mm
NPG 6804

Found guilty of high treason, Jane was initially spared execution, unlike her father-in-law John Dudley, Duke of Northumberland. Her fate was, however, sealed by her father's support for Sir Thomas Wyatt's rebellion in 1554 and she was beheaded at the Tower of London. No contemporary portrait of Lady Jane has been identified and it is possible that none was made during her lifetime.

Queen Mary I (1516–58)
Hans Eworth, 1554
Oil on panel, 216 x 169mm
NPG 4861

It is possible that this small, easily portable portrait was used to share Mary's likeness during the marriage negotiations with Philip II. Cruelly, Philip was said to have cursed the flattery of portrait painters when he first met Mary.

Jane Seymour (1508 or 1509–1537)
After Hans Holbein the Younger, c.1537
Oil on panel, 640 x 480mm
NPG 7025

This particularly decorative version of Hans Holbein's portrait of Jane Seymour, with its intricate chequered fabric, is unfinished. It is of a type that was commissioned by the Seymour family after Jane's death.

Opposite:
Anne Boleyn (c.1500–36)
Unidentified artist, late sixteenth century, based on a work of c.1533–6
Oil on panel, 543 x 416mm
NPG 668

Anne Boleyn was a patron of artists, with Hans Holbein designing gifts that she presented to Henry VIII, but no painted portrait survives from her time as queen.

the notion of a female successor: how could a queen rule, when society viewed women as inferior to men?

The primary role of England's queens had always been to secure the future of the dynasty by having sons. As she claimed the throne, Mary was aware that this was as true for a queen regnant as for a queen consort. It was the survival of four of Elizabeth of York's children beyond infancy that had done so much to ensure that the Tudors were still in power after half a century. By contrast, without sons, Mary had seen how vulnerable Katherine of Aragon and Anne Boleyn had become as their status in the king's eyes diminished. Ultimately, Henry VIII erased both women from the narrative of Tudor rule, stripping them of the title of queen as their marriages were declared void. Instead, Jane Seymour was celebrated as Elizabeth of York's successor and the model Tudor queen in Hans Holbein's great mural in Whitehall Palace. As the mother of the future Edward VI, it was Jane whom Henry considered to be his first queen and with whom he was buried in St George's Chapel, Windsor. It is therefore unsurprising that Mary and her councillors felt that it was imperative that she should marry.

Marriage also offered the monarch the chance to build alliances. The Tudor dynasty itself was founded on the most famous alliance in English history: the union of the houses of York and Lancaster that ended the Wars of the Roses through Henry VII's marriage to Elizabeth of York. However, choosing an English

Katherine Parr (1512–48)
Unidentified artist, c.1545
Oil on panel, 1803 x 940mm
NPG 4451

This impressive image uses expensive materials to convey Katherine Parr's lavish clothing and jewels, with extensive use of gold, silver and azurite. It is the earliest surviving full-length portrait of an English queen.

consort was not without risk, as it raised the prospect of competition within the aristocracy. This rivalry played out most obviously during the reign of Henry VIII. Titles and power flowed to the relations of Anne Boleyn, Jane Seymour, Katherine Howard and Katherine Parr as they rose in the king's favour, though all could fall away, and worse, if the marriage foundered. Such factional infighting could be mitigated by looking to other courts for a spouse, which also brought with it the greater prize of an international ally. It was the prospect of building a Protestant alliance with Germany that encouraged Thomas Cromwell to champion Anne of Cleves as Henry's new bride following the death of Jane Seymour. Consorts from foreign courts could also act as conduits for new fashions and ideas, although Anne of Cleves' lack of experience in the language of courtly love and performance that Henry favoured may have hampered their relationship from the beginning; their marriage lasted only six months. In choosing her husband, Mary learned from the experience of her much-married father. She avoided factional division by looking abroad, and, through her union with the Spanish King Philip II, she married a man in whose culture she had been raised by her mother. However, unlike the queens consort who had arrived in England from other countries over the centuries, Philip was coming not only to be the queen's subject, but also her superior within the institution of marriage.

This was the central challenge for a queen regnant: how to preserve the future of her dynasty without surrendering the power that she wielded to her husband. In this, the concept of the 'king's two bodies' offered a solution. The queen's corporeal body was human and, as a wife, was subordinate to her husband within their marriage, but as monarch she also embodied the body politic, and as such carried supreme authority within the realm. This distinction was reinforced at Mary's accession through The Queen Regent's Prerogative Act, which stated that Mary held the same power as that wielded by her male predecessors. However, Parliament could have no oversight over the way in which Mary herself chose to balance her identities as wife and queen. Thus, although the English Parliament built limitations on Philip's political power into the terms of the marriage contract with Spain, it was clear from the outset that Mary intended to rule jointly with her husband. English fears of Spanish intervention in English affairs, which prompted rebellion at the beginning of Mary's reign, were realised in 1558 when Philip succeeded in committing the country to support Spain's war with France. England subsequently lost Calais, its last territorial holding in France.

Mary's reign demonstrated the means by which a woman could rule while adhering to societal conventions. Even though the political arrangements for her marriage failed to work in practice, it is striking that on the accession of Elizabeth I, one of Parliament's first submissions to their new monarch was a request that she should marry. Assuming the throne aged only 25, where her half-sister Mary had been 37, all expectations were that the Tudor dynasty would continue through Elizabeth's marriage and children. However, Elizabeth rebuffed Parliament and her councillors in this matter, stating that it would be 'sufficient that a marble stone shall declare that a queen having reigned such a time lived and died a virgin'. Elizabeth used her unmarried status as a means of managing relationships both at home and abroad, entertaining suits from Eric XIV of Sweden, the Habsburg Archduke Charles of Austria, and both Henry III of France and his brother Hercule-François, Duke of Alençon, while also being widely expected to choose her long-standing favourite, Robert Dudley, Earl of Leicester. However, where Mary had hoped that marriage would stabilise her rule, Elizabeth's observations over the course of her childhood and during her sister's reign set her on a radically different path. By the time of her accession, Elizabeth also had first-hand experience of the personal risk that she could face through marriage. First, Thomas Seymour, whom Katherine Parr married after Henry VIII's death, took advantage of his position to try to force Elizabeth into marriage after Katherine's death in 1548. Then, at the beginning of Mary's reign, Protestant rebels in Kent plotted to marry Elizabeth to Edward Courtenay, Earl of

Queen Elizabeth I (1533–1603)
Unidentified artist, c.1560
Oil on panel, 394 x 273mm
NPG 4449

This modest early portrait of Elizabeth as queen is possibly of the same type as that sent to Catherine de' Medici, which prompted the French queen to exclaim, 'After what everyone tells me of her beauty, and after the paintings of her that I have seen, I must declare that she did not have good painters.'

Queen Elizabeth I (1533–1603)
Unidentified artist, c.1575
Oil on panel, 1130 x 787mm
NPG 2082

One of the most important surviving images of Elizabeth I, the face pattern derived from this portrait was used to produce images of the queen for many years.

Opposite:
Queen Elizabeth I (1533–1603)
Nicholas Hilliard, c.1575
Oil on panel, 787 x 610mm
National Museums Liverpool,
Walker Art Gallery, No. 2994

Known as the 'Pelican' portrait, this image exemplifies the transformation in Elizabeth's iconography that occurred in the 1570s as her councillors began to recognise that she might never marry. She is depicted wearing a jewel with a pelican plucking at its breast to feed its young, a Christian emblem of the Eucharist used to proclaim her own self-sacrifice and care for her subjects.

Devon, and place her on the throne in Mary's stead. On both occasions, Elizabeth faced the charge of treason. Thus, while unprecedented, her decision to rule alone was understood by those closest to her, with Robert Dudley remarking in 1566 that 'his true opinion was that she would never marry ... he knew her majesty as well or better than anyone else of her close acquaintance, for they had first become friends before she was eight years old. Both then and later (when she was old enough to marry) she said she never wished to do so.'

Mary and Elizabeth were not alone in navigating queenship in the mid-sixteenth century. By a quirk of fate, their reigns overlapped with Mary, Queen of Scots, and Jeanne III of Navarre, along with periods in which Mary of Guise and Catherine de' Medici acted as regents in Scotland and France. Coinciding with the bitter divisions of the Reformation, a number of Protestant theologians chose to attack queenship as embodied by the three Catholic Marys: Mary I, Mary of Guise and Mary, Queen of Scots. Most prominent of these was John Knox's *The First Blast of the Trumpet Against the Monstrous Regiment of Women*, published in 1558. Arguing that female rule was 'repugnant to Nature' and contrary to the Bible, Knox's poorly-timed book was coolly received by Elizabeth I. Knox held his line, but others found a means of accommodating Elizabeth's rule, not least for the fact that it would return England to Protestantism. As John Calvin wrote to Elizabeth's advisor William Cecil, Baron Burghley, although he had considered the 'government of women' to be 'a deviation from the original and proper order of nature', he was prepared to concede that an exceptional woman may be 'raised up by divine authority'. However, this exceptionalism had its limits; unlike her father and brother, Elizabeth claimed only the title 'Supreme Governor' of the church in England, rather than 'Supreme Head'. While the state could accommodate a woman at its head, the church could not.

Elizabeth's singular approach to queenship is documented through her portraits – even though she occasionally needed to be persuaded to participate in their production. Her ambivalence could perhaps relate to the way in which the portraits of her predecessors, both as queens consort, and her sister as queen regnant, were so closely identified with marriage: the portraits of Jane Seymour that had been created to pair with images of Henry VIII; the images of Anne of Cleves that were sent to England in advance of her arrival; and the counterpoint to these examples in the seemingly deliberate destruction of painted portraits of Anne Boleyn, of which only posthumous versions survive. Of Henry's queens, only Katherine Parr actively engaged in portraiture, commissioning works from a number of artists, and it is tempting to speculate as to whether her proactive self-presentation related to her attempt to secure the position of Governor during Edward VI's minority. Mary, by contrast, only briefly explored the possibilities of an iconography for a queen regnant. Once she had committed to marrying Philip II, her image was conceived in relation to his. This could be seen in the portrait commissioned from Philip's court artist, Anthonis Mor, which was reproduced in order to be shared with his family and with other courts, and which portrayed Mary seated in the manner of her predecessors as Habsburg queens consort. Most strikingly, the paired images of the royal couple that appeared on English coins and documents placed Philip in the dominant position on the left. At first, Elizabeth continued to use portraiture as a pragmatic tool for marriage negotiations, but over time, portraiture was freed to express new identities for the queen. As Elizabeth and her courtiers navigated her long reign, they used portraiture to place her into roles beyond that of wife and mother. In a court where performance permeated every aspect of life, drawing on classical sources, the Bible, encounters with other cultures through trade and exploration, and stories translated from across Europe, Elizabeth came to be revered not only as a queen, but as a goddess, an empress, and mother to the nation.

'We Princes Who Be Women': Catherine de' Medici in France

Susan Doran

Unlike Elizabeth I and Mary, Queen of Scots, Catherine de' Medici was not a reigning queen. For several brief periods she was named queen regent: short spells in the 1550s when her husband Henry II was on military campaigns; during the minority of her young son Charles IX from December 1560 until 1563; and for three months between Charles's death on 31 May 1574 and the return of his successor Henry III from Poland, where he had been the elected king. Catherine's status as regent followed earlier precedents in France, notably when Louise of Savoy assumed the role while her adult son, Francis I, was a captive in Spain. But, otherwise, Catherine's power and authority were informal and unusual, depending heavily on her relationship with her sons. Her influence was relatively weak during the reign of her eldest, Francis II, who looked to the Guise uncles of his wife Mary, Queen of Scots, for advice, but strong during the reigns of Charles IX and Henry III, who readily accepted their mother's prominence at court and in their counsels.

The careers of the three queens – Elizabeth, Mary, Queen of Scots, and Catherine – demonstrate that, within a patriarchal society, political power rested more easily on women who were single. Although Catherine was crowned and anointed when her husband Henry II succeeded to the throne in 1547, she remained outside the king's counsels for the whole of his reign and was consistently overshadowed by his *maîtresse en titre* Diane de Poitiers. Similarly, Mary had almost no power at all when married to Francis II, and she later struggled for pre-eminence over her second husband Henry, Lord Darnley, who wanted the crown matrimonial. Her third marriage to the earl of Bothwell triggered faction and brought about her deposition. Only during their periods of widowhood did Catherine and Mary come into their own. Mary then ruled Scotland successfully with the support of her kin; while Catherine exerted her authority, engaged in policymaking, and was viewed as a key political player in the governments of Charles IX and Henry III. For all the problems that arose from her single state, Elizabeth may have been wise not to marry.

Catherine understood instinctively that her authority depended on her not transgressing gender norms – the 'two bodies' theory of monarchical power could not apply to her as it did to Elizabeth and Mary – and she legitimised her political role in France by claiming it arose from her status as the widow and mother of kings. Fashioning her image as the devoted dowager queen, she never cast aside her black widow's weeds, though she made sure they were fashionably cut and luxuriously trimmed. For her *impresa*, she adopted images and mottos that drew attention to her grief at losing Henry, and she also appropriated the image of Artemisia, the dowager queen of ancient Caria, who had built the famous mausoleum at Halicarnassus for her dead husband. Imitating Artemisia, Catherine commissioned commemorative monuments for Henry II, including a grandiose mortuary chapel tomb in the abbey church of St-Denis. Emphasising her maternal role, Catherine became known as 'Reine Mère', and she explained her actions as arising from her motherly love for her royal sons and a duty to protect their patrimony by bringing order to the realm. Her counsel was fashioned as maternal advice; her dynastic plans fitted into a mother's responsibility to match-make for her children.

At the same time, Catherine, like Elizabeth and Mary, understood the importance of the Renaissance concept of 'magnificence' for rulers. 'Feminine' modesty was not appropriate for their roles, and they all used ceremony and the arts to bolster and project their own power. Unlike Elizabeth and Mary, Catherine also spent huge sums on building projects designed to impress. She built from scratch the Tuileries Palace, close to the Louvre, which became with its extensive gardens a site for royal entertainments. Also in Paris, Catherine rebuilt the Hôtel de la Reine as her main residence, which by the time of her death was a dazzling showcase for her vast collections of tapestries, portraits, metalwork, enamels, Limoges pottery and maps. It also contained a cabinet of mirrors, lined with 120 pieces of expensive Venetian mirror glass, probably the first of its kind in Europe. To pay for this royal magnificence, Catherine ran the crown into debt, a practice Elizabeth was determined to avoid.

Gendered language and stereotyping affected the reputations of all three queens. Catholics initially criticised Elizabeth as the weak prisoner of evil councillors; but she later was traduced as a Nero, a persecutory tyrant. Protestants labelled Mary as a Jezebel or Athalia. As for Catherine, she was hated by both Huguenots (French Protestants) and Ligueurs (Catholic partisans of the Guise family). In their literature, she was portrayed as a Machiavellian who used dark arts for her selfish ends. Protestants claimed that she had used poison – thought to be a woman's weapon – to assassinate her Huguenot enemy, the brother of Admiral Coligny. They also held Catherine complicit in the Massacre of St Bartholomew (23–4 August 1572), when Catholics slaughtered thousands of Huguenots who were in Paris for the wedding celebrations of her daughter and Henry of Navarre. League literature depicted her as a wicked manipulator who had usurped power from the king to satisfy her personal ambitions.

KATHARINA REGINA·HENRICI·ii·
VXOR, FRANCISCI CAROLI ET
HENRICI REGVM·MATER ·1579·

All three queens were also exposed to sexual slander. Mary was vilified as an adulteress and whore, as well as a murderer, while Elizabeth was rumoured to have given birth to bastards by her lover, Robert Dudley. Although Catherine's own chastity was not impugned, she was said to have used her ladies-in-waiting to seduce and spy on influential noblemen for her own political purposes. Catherine's Italian birth combined with her gender categorised her as a sexually deviant Florentine, who used 'feminine' skills of deception and manipulation to hold onto power. A 1573 poem written by a Huguenot called her a 'high born whore / the blood infected with the buggers of Italy'. The accusations against the queens were not based on evidence but on contemporary stereotypes of women as lascivious, untrustworthy, and unsuitable for rule. As Catherine herself commented: 'We princes who be women, of all persons, are subject to be slandered wrongfully of them that be our adversaries: other hurt they cannot do us.'

Catherine de' Medici (1519–89)
Marc Duval, 1579
Line engraving, 226 x 150mm
NPG D47413

Catherine de' Medici became dowager on the
death of her husband Henry II of France in July
1559. This engraving by the French printmaker
Marc Duval was produced in 1579, when Catherine's
son Henry III was king of France, and it depicts
her standing at a table with her hands on a closed
book. Behind her are Doric columns to the right,
and a landscape and castle visible through an open
window to the left. This image of the queen was
reproduced in later engravings.

Holding the Throne

From the very beginning of her reign, Elizabeth I had to confront the fact she had a rival: her cousin, Mary, Queen of Scots. Mary was the granddaughter of Henry VIII's sister Margaret and had ruled Scotland since infancy. Although excluded from the English line of succession by virtue of having been born outside the realm, Mary's claim was strengthened by the fact that, just as with Katherine of Aragon, Henry VIII had refused to recognise his marriage to Anne Boleyn. As a result, Elizabeth's legitimacy could be questioned. Henry VIII tried to unify the two branches of his family, and the kingdoms of England and Scotland, by marrying his son Edward to Mary. However, negotiations collapsed in the violence of the 'Rough Wooing', with English forces laying waste to Scottish territory on the borders, and Mary was sent to be raised by the Catholic family of her mother, Mary of Guise, in France. She married the heir to the French throne and was crowned queen of France in 1559 at the age of 16. However, her husband died only a year later and Mary returned to Scotland to rule her kingdom directly, and to assert her claim to the English throne. She quickly stepped back from an outright challenge to Elizabeth's rule but sought instead to be named heir presumptive. However, Elizabeth resisted legitimising Mary's claim, fearing that it would encourage those both at home and abroad

Mary, Queen of Scots (1542–87)
Unidentified artist, 1560s
Oil on panel, 251 x 191mm
NPG 1766

This portrait was produced during the period in which Mary sought to encourage Elizabeth to name her heir to the English throne; styling herself in correspondence as the queen's sister, who shared the experience of rule within the British Isles.

**William Cecil, 1st Baron Burghley
(1520 or 1521–98)**
Unidentified artist, *c.*1570
Oil on panel, 953 x 718mm
NPG 2184

Elizabeth called Burghley her 'spirit'; the origins
of Elizabeth's nicknames are not known, but they
were bestowed on those only within her most
intimate circle.

**George Talbot, 6th Earl of Shrewsbury
(c.1522–90)**
Unidentified artist, inscribed 1582
Black, brown and red chalk on paper, 330 x 225mm
NPG 6343

One of the wealthiest men in England, Talbot acted
as 'keeper' of Mary, Queen of Scots, between
1568 and 1585. This portrait bears a contemporary
inscription in French, and it is possible that it was
owned by one of the Scottish queen's supporters
in France.

who wished to see England return to Catholicism. And so the stage was set for an ongoing challenge to Elizabeth's authority.

In reality, there was little Elizabeth could do to prevent Mary becoming the focal point of plots against her rule, particularly given the disruption of the balance of power in Europe caused by religious division. In the 1560s, civil war broke out in France between Catholics and the Protestant Huguenots, while the Low Countries rebelled against Philip II of Spain's rule. As a result, conspiracies against Elizabeth drew in participants from Spain, Portugal, Italy and France, as Catholics sought to undermine Protestant rule in England as part of a broader means of reasserting Catholic dominance in Europe. This continued even as Mary's position in Scotland, which was also riven with religious conflict, became untenable. As with Elizabeth, the key question lay in deciding whom Mary would marry. After briefly entertaining the notion of marrying Elizabeth's favourite, Robert Dudley, Earl of Leicester – at the English queen's suggestion – Mary chose her cousin, Henry Stuart, Lord Darnley, and in 1566 they had a son, James. However, disaster followed. Darnley was murdered in 1567, and the man whom Mary married shortly afterwards, James Hepburn, Earl of Bothwell, was widely assumed to have been responsible. Mary was forced to abdicate in favour of her son, and fled to England to seek Elizabeth's protection. It was at this point that Mary's potency as a rallying point for Catholics was demonstrated. She could pose no practical threat: she was a queen stripped of her kingdom, with a son who was being raised as a Protestant, and was under house arrest in the kingdom of her rival. Nonetheless, the Northern Earls rose in rebellion to support Mary's claim in 1569, and the papal bull *Regnans in excelsis*, excommunicating Elizabeth I in 1570, inspired the Ridolfi plot of 1571, which resulted in the execution of the premier nobleman in England, Thomas Howard, Duke of Norfolk. As Elizabeth's reign moved into its second decade and Mary was imprisoned under the supervision of George Talbot, Earl of Shrewsbury, Elizabeth's three most prominent councillors, William Cecil, Robert Dudley and

Sir Francis Walsingham, each attempted to protect their queen and secure the Protestant Reformation in England.

William Cecil, Baron Burghley, was Elizabeth's longest-standing advisor, her first Secretary of State and then Lord Treasurer. From this position he advocated for the most obvious solution to the threat that Mary posed as heir, which was for Elizabeth to marry and have a child. As Elizabeth entered her forties, this became less and less likely. However, Burghley threw his full support behind one final possibility: marriage to Catherine de' Medici's fourth son, Hercule-François, Duke of Alençon. Burghley held out hope that Elizabeth still might have a child, but more immediately, that an alliance would undermine any attempt by the Spanish to work with the Catholic royal family in France against the English. The challenge facing English diplomats in the febrile religious atmosphere of these years was brutally demonstrated in 1572. In that year, the Treaty of Blois, which established an alliance against the Spanish and prevented the French from supporting Mary, Queen of Scots, was almost immediately negated by the massacre of Huguenots who had gathered in Paris to celebrate the marriage of the Protestant King Henry IV of Navarre to Marguerite, the French king's

Francis Bacon, 1st Viscount St Alban (1561–1626)
Nicholas Hilliard, 1578
Watercolour and bodycolour on vellum laid on card, 60 x 47mm
NPG 6761

This portrait was produced while Francis Bacon was part of the entourage of the English ambassador to France along with the artist Nicholas Hilliard. Aged only 18, Bacon was gaining his first experience of the practice of diplomacy, carrying information relating to the marriage negotiations between Elizabeth and Alençon for Burghley, Dudley and Walsingham.

Robert Dudley, 1st Earl of Leicester
(1532 or 1533–88)
Unidentified artist, *c*.1575
Oil on panel, 1080 x 826mm
NPG 447

This glamorous portrait may have been produced
as part of the elaborate festivities that Leicester
hosted at Kenilworth in 1575 as part of a final
attempt to secure the queen's hand in marriage.

Mary, Queen of Scots (1542–87)
After Nicholas Hilliard, inscribed 1578
Oil on panel, 791 x 902mm
NPG 429

The inscription records that Mary had been a
prisoner for ten years at the time this likeness was
produced. She prominently displays her rosary,
which incorporates a Latin motto that can be
translated as 'Troubles on all sides'.

Sir Philip Sidney (1554–86)
Unidentified artist, *c.*1576
Oil on panel, 1139 x 840mm
NPG 5732

The Latin motto on this portrait may well have been added after Sidney's death; it can be translated as 'The rest is fame'.

Robert Sidney, 1st Earl of Leicester (1563–1626)
Daniël van den Queborn, *c.*1588
Oil on canvas, 991 x 794mm
NPG 1862

A number of English soldiers in the Low Countries commissioned their portrait from Queborn. The inscribed motto *inveniam viam aut faciam* translates to 'I shall either find a way or make one'.

sister. The English were left trying to find a means of securing a powerful ally against the Spanish without endorsing the persecution of French Protestants or French ambitions to expand their territory into the Netherlands. It was this that marriage to Alençon offered in 1578, and despite their age difference it seems that both Elizabeth and Hercule-François committed to the performance of their courtship. The miniaturist Nicholas Hilliard was despatched to Paris in the entourage of the new English ambassador to make a portrait of the duke for Elizabeth, and Alençon himself travelled to England in 1581. However, not all Elizabeth's advisors were convinced and popular opinion raged against the idea of Elizabeth marrying a French Catholic after the St Bartholomew's Day massacre. The marriage could not proceed, and with the end of this possibility, it was harder to resist what William Cecil had hoped to avoid: English military involvement on the continent.

It had long been clear that any military threat to England from Spain would come via the Low Countries. Charles V had inherited control of the region in 1506 and passed it to his son Philip II on Philip's marriage to Mary Tudor, in order to use the alliance with England to counter French ambitions in the region. All changed with the accession of Elizabeth I, and when William of Orange instigated a Protestant revolt against Spanish rule in 1568, it became clear that the increased Spanish military presence in the region could easily be directed against England once the rebels had been defeated. The arrival of Philip's half-brother, John of Austria, as Governor-General fuelled the fear that the Spanish would use their base in the Low Countries to support plots to liberate Mary, Queen of Scots, and place her on the throne. The rebellious United Provinces in the north looked to Protestant England for support, but Elizabeth initially rebutted all overtures, aware that aiding a rebellion against Philip would hardly support her case that he had no right to support rebels in England. However, as Spain formed an alliance with the Catholic League in France and the rebels surrendered Antwerp, Elizabeth was forced into action. She turned to her longstanding favourite, Robert Dudley, Earl of Leicester, to lead an English expeditionary force in support of the rebels. However, isolated and without a clear mandate, Leicester made the fateful decision to accept the position of Governor-General of the Netherlands. Elizabeth was appalled and ordered him to resign. Attempting to combine political and military authority, while also heeding the queen's instruction to fight a defensive war, Leicester's intervention with the English forces failed to have a decisive impact on the Spanish.

Leicester returned to England burdened by personal debts from the campaign and with a damaged reputation. He had failed at one of the chief responsibilities of the ideal courtier, namely 'to undertake his bold feats and courageous enterprises in war'. He was not alone; a generation of young men had seized the opportunity offered by the military campaign to try to demonstrate their personal valour and skill in command. Chief among these were Leicester's nephews, Philip and Robert Sidney. Both had travelled extensively in Europe in order to build networks and learn the skills of leadership. Many hoped that Philip, the elder of the two, could become a unifying leader of the Protestant factions scattered across Europe. Named after his Catholic godfather, Philip II of Spain, Philip's ardent Protestantism and hostility to the French had only been strengthened by his personal experience of the St Bartholomew's Day massacre, which took place while he was staying with his future father-in-law Francis Walsingham in Paris. On his return to England, he had come to embody the ideal Renaissance courtier, a cultivated poet counsellor to the queen, at the centre of a network of scholars, writers, diplomats and politicians. However, from the start, Philip was disillusioned by the campaign in the Netherlands and held out little hope for success. He left his regiment, and it was as an independent soldier that he took part in a raid on a Spanish supply convoy on the morning of 22 September 1586. He was wounded in the leg and died from gangrene nearly four weeks later, triggering an outpouring of public grief from his fellow soldiers, writers and courtiers.

As Sidney lay dying, an alternative solution to the problem of Mary, Queen of Scots, was reaching its conclusion. Long convinced that Mary would always pose a threat to Elizabeth, Walsingham had advocated for the Scottish queen's execution for years. When he became aware of a plot by a group of young Catholics at court to assassinate Elizabeth he allowed it to continue. Their leader, Anthony Babington, had first encountered the Scottish queen when serving as a page in the household of her custodian, George Talbot, Earl of Shrewsbury; he had then developed contacts with Mary's supporters in Paris. Walsingham monitored Mary's correspondence with Babington through double agents and waited to act until she had incriminated herself by endorsing Elizabeth's assassination and acknowledging the plan that she should be rescued and protected until the Spanish army arrived. This was the unequivocal evidence of treason that could be used to justify the execution of a queen. However, it took the combined effort of all three of Elizabeth's most trusted advisors, Burghley, Leicester and Walsingham, to convince the queen first to summon Parliament and then to sign the warrant for Mary's execution. The drawn-out process allowed the English to assess the risk from Mary's allies in Scotland and France, and also distanced Elizabeth from the act itself: it was Parliament that passed the death sentence and her councillors who moved to act swiftly once the warrant was signed, removing any opportunity for her to offer clemency to her cousin. Walsingham was proved correct, and at Mary's death the plots against Elizabeth ceased. However, the Spanish threat to the nation remained.

Anthony Babington and the Memorialisation of a Conspiracy

Charlotte Bolland

In 1586, a young Catholic courtier visited the studio of the goldsmith and picturemaker Robert Peake to commission a number of portraits as a 'memorial of so worthy an act as attempting her Majesties person'. Anthony Babington was the leader of a plot to assassinate Elizabeth I and free Mary, Queen of Scots, placing the Scottish queen on the English throne with the support of a joint invasion by the Spanish and the Catholic League in France. Initially, he requested that his image should bear a Latin inscription that acknowledged his co-conspirators with the words 'These men are my companions, whom very dangers draw'; he then requested that this be changed to 'To what end are these things to men that hasten to another purpose'. The portraits are not known to survive, but they may perhaps one day be found among the small head-and-shoulder depictions of unidentified young men from the 1580s that are attributed to Peake. Elizabeth almost certainly saw the portraits; a warrant in December 1588 paid Peake 'for making of vj several pictures of Babington, Tichbourne, Barnewell and other Traytors for special cause concerning her majesties service' in August 1586, after the conspiracy had been uncovered. These were unlikely to have been the original paintings, which were apparently stored in Babington's lodgings and were still being searched for in Catholic households in London after Babington's arrest, but rather copies made from Peake's preparatory drawings.

Although Babington's own enquiries had shown that most English Catholics were likely to support the government in the event of an invasion by the French and Spanish, the assassination plan itself was plausible; these were men who could get close enough to the queen to strike a fatal blow. On seeing the portraits Elizabeth recognised Robert Barnewell from his attendance at court in the service of the earl of Kildare, while Babington provided John Savage, a former soldier who had served with the duke of Parma in the Netherlands, with money for clothes; Savage was aware that in his own apparel 'shall I never come near the Queen'. Just as he used the conspirators to entrap Mary, Queen of Scots, Walsingham seems to have used their portraits to manipulate Elizabeth's response. This was the first Catholic plot in which the queen's assassination formed an integral part from its conception.

By bringing Elizabeth face to face with the men who planned to kill her, it was likely hoped that she could be encouraged into a visceral emotional response that would override her reluctance to physically harm Mary, something that had frustrated Walsingham on repeated occasions. In this, the portraits seem to have been effective; Babington and the first six co-conspirators were executed particularly cruelly and Elizabeth agreed to Mary's trial for treason.

Walsingham's network of double agents and informers, which reached across Europe to Paris and Rome, and as far as Moscow and Constantinople, has earned him the reputation as the founding father of the secret service: Elizabeth's, and England's, first spymaster. His orchestration of the Babington Plot utilised all the skills that he had developed over nearly two decades in royal service. The crucial double agent was Gilbert Gifford, who seems to have made contact with Walsingham's agents in Rome and to have been in Walsingham's service by the time he returned to England with a letter of recommendation to Mary from her agent in Paris. Walsingham used him to convey Mary's correspondence, with an elaborate system devised by which her letters were smuggled within barrels of beer, in order to fool Mary into thinking that all was concealed from the English authorities. Mary communicated using ciphers, but Walsingham had his own codebreaker, Thomas Phelippes. He could therefore not only decipher the evidence of Mary's treason, as she advised Babington to 'set the six gentlemen to work', but also use the letters to gain more information about the plot, adding a postscript purporting to be from Mary to request the names of the six men who planned to assassinate Elizabeth.

With the loss of the portraits with which Babington and his co-conspirators sought to make their memorial, it is an image of Walsingham that now serves as the most potent allegory of his victory over the Catholic threats to Elizabeth in the 1580s. For a man who conducted so much of his work for the queen in secrecy, it is perhaps not surprising that Walsingham's portraits should appear modest. He is depicted soberly dressed in black in his two known portrait types, with little adornment; Elizabeth's devoutly Protestant servant whom she nicknamed her 'Moor' who 'cannot change his colour'. However, much like the secret writing technology of Walsingham's master forger Arthur Gregory, there is one portrait that has had its secrets revealed through technology. X-radiography and infrared reflectograpy, which provide images of what lies beneath the surface, have revealed that one small-scale painting, of Walsingham's head only, was painted over a devotional image of the Virgin and Child. The circumstances in which this painting was produced are not known. It was quite probably the result of a resourceful artist reusing an unsold work from the studio in order to reduce costs. However, the tantalising possibility exists that it was deliberate. At a time when portraits were playing a role in one of the most dramatic Catholic plots against England's virgin queen, how fitting that an artist should produce a portrait of her spymaster that erased an archetypal Catholic devotional image of the Virgin and Child.

Sir Francis Walsingham (c.1532–90)
Unidentified artist, c.1585
Oil on panel, 375 x 298mm
NPG 1704

The Virgin and Child with Two Angels
Hans Memling, 1480–90
Oil on panel, 360 x 260mm
Prado Museum P002543

The images produced by x-radiography and
infrared reflectography suggest that the image
beneath the portrait of Francis Walsingham is
of a similar composition to this small devotional
painting. The Virgin and Child are shown in an
enclosed garden accompanied by angels; it was
a composition that was popularised by artists
working in the Low Countries.

Gerlach Flicke (active 1545, d.1558)
and Henry Strangeways (d.1562)
Gerlach Flicke, 1554
Oil on paper laid on panel, 88 x 119mm
NPG 6353

The inscription records that this double portrait
was produced while both men were in prison: 'One
prisoner, for thother, hath done this.' It is not known
why Flicke was imprisoned, but the Latin inscription
above his portrait suggests that he feared for his
life, painting himself using a mirror 'for his dear
friends ... that they might have something by which
to remember him after his death'.

Piracy, Privateering and Trade

In 1553, the Imperial ambassador Jean Scheyfve reported on a case of piracy by the 'notorious personage' Henry Strangeways. The Englishman had seized a vessel containing wool, money and wine belonging to the Emperor, landing in the Scilly Isles before fleeing to Ireland and then to France. Edward VI and his council promised to make an example of Strangeways, and Scheyfve reassured the letter's recipient that the authorities had 'exerted themselves so diligently that the like has never before been witnessed in England, and the pirates and sea-robbers will be stricken with salutary fear'. However, Scheyfve's confidence in the English authorities proved to be misplaced. Strangeways returned to England of his own volition the following year with two vessels laden with arms, and was able to throw himself on Mary I's mercy. He spent time in the Tower, but eventually gained his freedom through bribery and was able to settle the Spanish claims of piracy against him. During his time in prison, his portrait was painted by a fellow prisoner, the German artist Gerlach Flicke. Dressed in black with long red hair and a full beard, this is Strangeways 'the Rover', the lute-playing pirate from Dorset. On his release, Strangeways' ambition was undiminished and he hoped to 'steal an island' from the king of Spain; ultimately there was opportunity enough to raid Spanish and Portuguese ships closer to home. Nevertheless, piracy was still a crime and when Strangeways was apprehended off the French coast and returned to London, he was sentenced to death. By this point, Elizabeth I was queen and her realm was under threat on a number of fronts. Sailors who were skilled in skirmishes at sea had a value that could place them above the law; Strangeways was pardoned. He was subsequently appointed a captain in the relief of English and Huguenot soldiers in France. Here his luck ran out; he was mortally

ADVAVNCEMENT BY DILLIGE

Sr Iohn Hawkins Knight

His shadow to the world brave Hawkins showes,
Who was a Bulwark to his frinds, to foes
Resistles Thunder; who for countries sake
So many a hard attempt durst vndertake
That Indian in their barbarous tongues do praise him,
And vnto Heauen his very foes doe raise him.
He in his life whole Seas could boldly tame,
Let not then Lethes Reuer drowne his name. A.H.

wounded as he attempted to cross the French lines, memorialised in a ballad that encapsulates the shifting position of the 'rovers' of the seas around the British Isles:

> For by legall lawes he was condemd,
> Yet mercy bare the mace,
> And in respect he wold amend,
> He found a princes grace.

Strangeways was among the first of Elizabeth's 'Sea Dogs'. These were the men who made their careers at sea, seeking new opportunities for financial reward beyond the realm through piracy, privateering and trade. Where the penalty for piracy was death, these men were able to act with impunity, as their quest for personal gain aligned with the queen's need to counter the threats first from France and then from Spain, both militarily and financially. With the 'Sea Dogs' intercepting Spanish ships bearing gold from their colonies in South America, disrupting Spanish trading monopolies and wreaking havoc in the Caribbean, Elizabeth was able to profit at the expense of Philip II, while a generation of men honed their skills in naval conflict, navigation and exploration. These were the skills that England needed for defence and for expansion. They would underpin both the country's emergence as a sea power and its colonial enterprises in Ireland and America. Utilising the skills of individuals who wished to seek personal gain in the queen's name suited Elizabeth's approach to conflict, as she was able to challenge Spain at sea without deploying the English navy. Official sanction from the queen and her councillors, in the form of letters of marque and

Sir John Hawkins (1532–95)
Robert Boissard, c.1597–1601
Engraving, 189 x 130mm
NPG D48075

investment in the voyages, transformed the English sea captains from pirates to privateers. In the eyes of the Spanish, and those they encountered at sea, and in Africa and the Caribbean, the most infamous of these were the cousins John Hawkins and Francis Drake.

Raised in the same household in Plymouth, Hawkins was Drake's senior by eight years. It was on Hawkins' ships as a young man in his early twenties that Drake first observed the freedom with which a captain could operate when far from the centres of both English and Spanish authority. Hawkins had set his sights on disrupting the Spanish and Portuguese monopolies in the lucrative trade in enslaved people between the west coast of Africa and the Caribbean. He took to referring to the Spanish king as 'my old master' while claiming to have performed useful service for Spanish emissaries in Plymouth. This was intended to lend an air of legitimacy to his first slaving voyage in 1562, in which he paid Spanish customs charges on the more than three hundred people whom he captured and trafficked across the Atlantic to Hispaniola. Hawkins' hopes of gaining official permission to participate in the trade of enslaved people were not realised; the homeward cargo that he sent to Seville, the seat of the Spanish colonial administration, was confiscated and the Spanish colonists in the Caribbean were barred from trading with the English. However, in financial terms, the voyage was a success.

Despite, or perhaps because of, Spanish antagonism, Hawkins' second and third slaving voyages were undertaken under the supervision of William Cecil, Baron Burghley, with investment from a number of privy councillors. It is estimated that Hawkins trafficked more than a thousand people from West Africa to the Caribbean over the course of three voyages. The venture also secured the queen's support, with ships chartered from the navy sailing under the royal standard, and the grant of a coat of arms to Hawkins in reward for the money that he brought back to England. Hawkins' third voyage exemplified the duplicitous approach that the English were taking to engagements with Spain, with the privy council barring Hawkins from engaging in the trade of enslaved people to assuage Spanish anger at the challenge to their monopoly, while continuing to provide practical support. However, it was to prove to be the last English slaving voyage in the sixteenth century. Hawkins' ships suffered heavy losses off the coast of Mexico after an encounter with the Spanish plate fleet, during which Drake fled in the darkness on the *Judith*; Hawkins eventually made it back to England on the *Minion*, but with only fifteen men. As Anglo-Spanish relations deteriorated, the English shifted from their disreputable, but deniable, disruption of trade to direct attacks on Spanish treasure ships, and on Spanish colonial towns and cities across the Caribbean.

It was in this arena that Francis Drake gained his legendary reputation across Europe and its colonies: El Draque, Franciscus Draco, the Dragon. He returned repeatedly to the Caribbean, raiding Spanish settlements alongside English and French pirates. In 1572 he attacked Nombre de Dios, the port at which the Spanish fleet loaded the gold that arrived by land from Panama City. It was during this engagement that Diego, who had been enslaved in the household of the captain general of the town, joined Drake's ship. In a striking example of the potency of shared enmity, Diego was able to broker an alliance between Drake and the Cimarrons, Africans who had escaped from slavery and regularly harried the Spanish settlements. The subsequent joint attack on the Spanish treasure transport made Drake a wealthy man. He returned to Plymouth, with Diego, to buy property and with the resources to set up as a merchant. While his activities were tacitly condoned by the English authorities, he was not yet a figure at court. It was investment in the attempt of Walter Devereux, Earl of Essex, to occupy Antrim in Ulster that brought Drake the connections that would transform his ambitions. Conversations with Sir Francis Walsingham resulted in a plan to raid Spanish settlements in the Pacific. Ostensibly a trading venture, the details of the programme of piracy were kept secret from a number of the participants. Unbeknownst to them, the crew who set sail with Drake in

1577, including Diego as Drake's personal manservant, were setting out on an extraordinary three-year circumnavigation. Drake's raids across the Pacific and Indian Oceans demonstrated to the Spanish that it was not only their settlements in the Caribbean that were threatened by the English, and also delivered an almost unimaginable bounty to the queen. Publically Elizabeth professed embarrassment at Drake's activities; privately, she was the only person to whom Drake confided the details of his cargo. Much of it was unregistered, as many of the ships that Drake raided had attempted to evade Spanish levies and, without an inventory, it was difficult for the Spanish to claim restitution.

Drake modelled his performance as a sea captain on that of his cousin John Hawkins, wearing fine silk, dining on silver plate and insisting that any personal attack on him constituted an attack on the queen herself. It is not hard to imagine his delight, therefore, when the queen knighted him after his circumnavigation. He quickly commissioned a portrait from his fellow West Countryman, Nicholas Hilliard, which captured his stocky frame and ruddy features, and his extraordinary wealth in the form of a thick gold chain, as he joined the country's elite. Both Drake and Hawkins explicitly referenced the exploits that had elevated them in the queen's eyes in their choice of crests for their coats of arms. Hawkins requested that a bound African man should adorn his coat of arms, while Drake had a ship drawn around the world with divine assistance. After the elevation of their social status, both men worked more closely with the English authorities. While Drake was raiding in the Caribbean, Hawkins was engaged in counter-espionage, offering his fleet in support of Spanish plans to place Mary, Queen of Scots, on the English throne, and reporting any information that he gleaned

Sir Francis Drake (1540–96)
Nicholas Hilliard, 1581
Watercolour on vellum, 28mm (diameter)
NPG 4851

Sten wick

Auspicante   Jehouah

Robert Boissard fc

Captaine Christopher Carleill Esquire

At any time if Carleill led a fleete,
Neptune would lay his trident at his feete,
And when by land his powers he did advaunce,
Mars himself would be glad to bow ats' launce,
Let then both Land and Sea his fame forth tell,
Who both on Sea and Land defend so well.

to Burghley. Despite his popularity with the queen, Drake remained a less than reputable figure at court; Burghley reportedly rejected a gift of ten gold bars on the grounds that they were stolen goods. However, Drake was not short of investors when planning a raid on the West Indies in 1584 to intercept the Spanish treasure fleet. Elizabeth retained the right to disavow his activities, as the planned attack amounted to an act of war against Spain, with the fleet including a military force commanded by Christopher Carleill, Walsingham's stepson. Drake failed to capture the treasure fleet, but occupied and destroyed the towns of Santo Domingo and Cartagena as well as the fort at San Augustín. He returned without treasure, but having demonstrated that he posed perhaps the greatest individual threat to Spanish maritime power.

The enormous profits available through raids in the Caribbean proved irresistible to both Hawkins and Drake. They sailed together again as joint commanders of a venture that left Plymouth in 1595. It was to be a fatal temptation; both succumbed to illness in quick succession and were buried in the Caribbean seas on which they had made their careers. However, by that point they had achieved a form of immortality, with the skills that they had honed against the Spanish in the Caribbean written into history in the defence of the realm against the Spanish Armada.

Christopher Carleill (1551?–1593)
Robert Boissard, c.1593–1603
Engraving, 204 x 145mm
NPG D21248

As with many of his contemporaries, Carleill's career combined the roles of soldier, naval officer and merchant. The inscription 'Sten Wick' on this portrait records Carleill's service in the city at the time it was beseiged by the Spanish. His grandfather co-founded the Muscovy Company and, in 1582, Carleill commanded a squadron of ships that escorted merchants to Russia and returned with a Russian envoy to Elizabeth I.

Diego, Drake and Piracy in Panama

Cassander L. Smith

In the popular British imagination, Sir Francis Drake is a daring sixteenth-century privateer who achieved brazen raids on Spanish-controlled islands in the Caribbean and circumnavigated the world in 1577. He is also remarkable for the alliances he forged during his high-seas ventures and the narratives produced about those ventures. One narrative in particular, *Sir Francis Drake Revived* (1626), records his escapades on the Isthmus of Panama in 1572–3, where he spent the better part of a year hiding out in various nooks and crannies along the Panama coast, biding his time. Drake's mission? To rob Spanish mule trains of their gold, silver, pearls and other valuables confiscated out of mines along the west coast of South America. Acting on the advice of a Black African informant named Diego, Drake aligned his efforts with a band of Cimarrons, formerly enslaved Africans who had run away from their Spanish enslavers and built settlements in the Panamanian mountains and jungles. With the help of Cimarrons, Drake carried out his raid in April 1573. He escaped Panama with enough loot to fill the cargo holds of two ships.

The narrative of the piratical adventure *Sir Francis Drake Revived* is especially intriguing because it names and features several Black Africans, among them Diego, who was a scout, negotiator, and later personal groom for Drake. The first time readers are introduced to Diego in Drake's narrative is like a scene from a Quentin Tarantino movie – lots of gunfire and chaos with a smattering of grotesque humour. The scene begins when Drake and fifty of his men land on the coast of Nombre de Dios. Despite some Spanish resistance, they take the town and hold it from a strategic location in the marketplace. It is raining. The cobblestone streets are slick and muddy. Drake and his men must hold the town. At stake, they believe, is a huge store of silver and gold they expect to find in the governor's storehouse. One can imagine Drake shouting to be heard over the rain pelting the streets while he organises his men into a defensive formation.

Meanwhile, another scene unfolds back on the beach, where Drake has left his ships and a score of men to guard them. On the beach, an enslaved man sees the ships and calls out to them, asking whether the ships belong to Drake. One of the crewmen shouts back an affirmation. At that point, the enslaved man runs towards the ships. Alarmed, the crewmen fire on the man, who it turns out is seeking refuge with Drake. This is, of course, Diego. None of the bullets hit Diego, so he keeps running in the direction of the ships, 'intreating to be taken aboard'. The crew allows him to board. Frantically, Diego warns them that more Spanish troops are on the way and implores Drake and his men to retreat.

One of the sailors relays this message to Drake. Before Drake can act on this report, he faints. As it turns out, he was shot in the initial battle for Nombre de Dios. The men carry Drake back to the ships. They row away from the beach with the occasional forlorn glance back at Nombre de Dios and all that silver and gold they think they have left behind. Importantly, Diego is with them, having decided to cast his fate with the English.

The narrative provides minimal biographical information about Diego. We know nothing about how he came to be enslaved in Panama. The narrative does not even record his direct speech. All his deeds and words are paraphrased, mediated by others. Based on that mediation, we do learn that Diego harboured a particular animosity towards his Spanish enslavers. Drake explains to readers that Diego hates the Spanish because they used him in their campaigns against the Cimarrons, and now the Cimarrons want to kill Diego. Diego, then, according to Drake, seeks his protection from both the Cimarrons and the Spanish. In *Sir Francis Drake Revived*, Diego appears a refugee and Drake a great liberator. The reader, however, would do well to approach Diego's characterisation with more circumspection, as certain incidents in the narrative point to a complex set of motives for Diego. As one example, it is Diego who first suggests to Drake that he seek out the Cimarrons to stage his raid of mule-trains. The suggestion of an English–Cimarron alliance enables Diego to curry favour not just with the English but also with the Cimarrons. This recommendation, then, is no more disinterested than Diego's insistence that Drake abandon Nombre de Dios, a move that also takes him, Diego, away from the town and his Spanish enslavers. When Drake departed Panama in 1573, he took Diego with him. Diego later travelled with Drake on his circumnavigation, and died two years into the voyage.

Le Forge Roialle Et Ordinaire Ou Se Font Lor Prouenant Des Mynes (*The Royal or Ordinary Forge Where the Gold Coming From the Mines is Made*) from *Histoire Naturelle des Indes* (f. 102r)
Unidentified artist, c.1586
Illustrated manuscript, 293 x 197mm
The Morgan Library MA3900

Leport Appelle' Le Nombre De Dieu (*The Port Called Nombre De Dios*) from *Histoire Naturelle des Indes* (f. 97r)
Unidentified artist, c.1586
Illustrated manuscript, 293 x 197mm
The Morgan Library MA3900

The French inscription reads: 'This is a beautiful and spacious harbour having a depth of seven to eight fathoms of water in which the fleet of ships from Spain arrives to trade merchandise with those from Peru which is located in a mountainous region where the air is heavy and unhealthy and the Spaniard cannot live there for a long time.'

Le port appellé le nombre de dieu

Ce port est ung beau haure e spacieux tirant sept a huict brasses deaue
auquel arriuent les flottes des nauires despaignol pour traicte marchandise
aut ceux du piron eft am scituee en ung lieux montaigneux et duquel
lair est fort greua de mal sain ny pouuant durer longtemps les espaignolz

The Spanish and English Armadas

Like most sixteenth-century rulers, Philip II of Spain believed in providence and in his personal agency, and responsibility, for the realisation of a divine plan. After he had helped to bring England back into the Catholic fold through his marriage to Mary I, England's return to Protestantism under Elizabeth I was a personal affront, particularly as he had protected Elizabeth from charges of treason while king of England. During that time, he had believed that marrying Elizabeth to a Catholic prince would be the safest means by which to ensure that Spain retained influence in England, as Elizabeth's execution would simply clear the way for Mary, Queen of Scots, to become heir to the English throne with the full support of the French. However, as the alliance between Scotland and France waned after Mary's return to Scotland and it became clear that Elizabeth and her councillors were constructing a religious settlement that would stabilise the Protestant Church in England, Philip came to see Mary, Queen of Scots, as 'the most suitable instrument' for the restoration of Catholicism in England and Scotland. As Elizabeth was well aware, this remained the case in the immediate aftermath of Mary's execution, for the taint of regicide offered ideal justification for a Spanish attack. In reality, the provocative actions by the Protestant English in the Netherlands and the Caribbean had long provided justification enough in Spanish eyes, and preparations for an invasion were well underway. Instead

King Philip II of Spain (1527–98)
Unidentified artist, c.1580
Oil on canvas, 1842 x 1041mm
NPG 347

Sir Francis Drake (1540–96)
Unidentified artist, c.1581
Oil on panel, 1813 x 1130mm
NPG 4032

Henry Stanley, 4th Earl of Derby (1531–93)
Unidentified artist, late sixteenth century
Oil on panel, 610 x 495mm
NPG 7000

of the Queen of Scots, Philip would place his daughter Isabella on the English throne, for, as the English Lord High Admiral Charles Howard warned Sir Francis Walsingham, 'there is no question but the King of Spain hath engaged his honour to the uttermost in this, for the overthrow of her Majesty and this realm'.

A proxy war continued for another year as the Spanish readied their forces and the English tried to buy time. Two months after Mary's execution, Francis Drake sailed for the Spanish coast to attack Spanish ships at sea and in port. He had the queen's blessing but, as ever, Elizabeth prevaricated in order to absolve herself of personal responsibility, sending a message after Drake to rescind her initial instruction; it was never received. The raid played to Drake's skills. He did not seek to engage the Spanish fleet in open battle but instead headed to Cádiz, taking the lightly defended port by surprise. Over two dozen Spanish ships were plundered and burned, setting back preparations for an invasion by a year. Drake continued onwards into Portuguese waters and on to the Azores where he took the *San Felipe*. It was on a voyage from Goa to Lisbon, with a cargo of porcelain, silks, velvet and jewels, and, as a ship that personally belonged to Philip, added insult to injury as Drake returned to England to crow about the 'singeing of the King of Spain's beard' in Cádiz. Elizabeth apologised to the Spanish for the raid and professed to be 'greatly offended' by Drake's actions. Such protestations fooled no one. However, disingenuousness was not the sole preserve of the English. Both sides were aware that the Spanish troops in the Netherlands posed the greatest threat to England, and the Spanish were happy to entertain the English delegates who travelled to Ostend in January 1588 in hopes of a negotiated peace. While Elizabeth's chief commissioner, Henry Stanley, Earl of Derby, treated with Philip's nephew Alessandro Farnese, Duke of Parma, all prepared for an invasion. The troops of Robert Dudley, Earl of Leicester, were brought back from the Netherlands, England's coastal defences were strengthened, and the navy was placed under the command of Charles Howard, Earl of Nottingham, with Francis Drake at his side; Parma readied the barges that would ferry troops across the

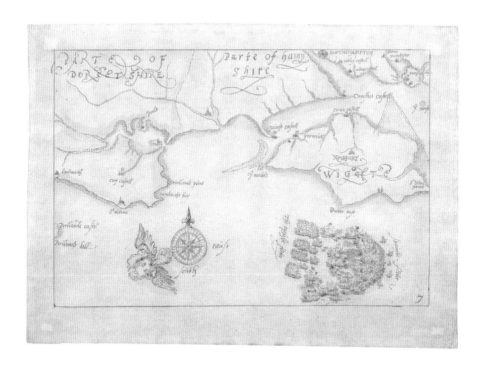

Armada Map: The English and Spanish Fleets Engaging off the Isle of Wight, 4 August 1588
Unidentified artist, c.1589
Pen and ink with watercolour on linen rag, 270 x 370mm
National Museum of the Royal Navy
NMRN 2020/43/7

Queen Elizabeth I (1533–1603)
Unidentified artist, c.1588
Oil on panel, 978 x 724mm
NPG 541

This is one of three surviving versions of the so-called 'Armada' portrait of Elizabeth I. The horizontal alignment of the boards suggests that it was originally in a landscape format, similar to the other two versions. It has been cut down to a standard portrait format at some point in its history.

Channel, and the Spanish fleet set off from A Coruña. On 19 July, beacons lit up across southern England as the Armada was sighted off Lizard Point.

The battle that took place as the Spanish fleet headed to the Netherlands to join Parma and his invasion army has passed into English legend. Squadrons under the command of Howard, Drake, John Hawkins and Martin Frobisher engaged the Spanish along the south coast of England and across the Channel, sending fire ships to scatter the fleet off Gravelines. The English feared the Spanish would regroup and Leicester was appointed to lead the troops against a land invasion. It was at Tilbury, on the north bank of the river Thames, that Elizabeth gave the speech that would shape the narrative of English sovereignty for centuries:

> I know I have the body but of a weak and feeble woman; but I have the heart and stomach of a king, and of a king of England too, and think foul scorn that Parma or Spain, or any prince of Europe, should dare to invade the borders of my realm ... we shall shortly have a famous victory over those enemies of my God, of my kingdom, and of my people.

As Elizabeth spoke, the threat had already passed. Storms had forced the Spanish to travel northwards around Scotland and Ireland; the heaviest Spanish losses were off the west coast of Ireland, long after the English had ceased to pursue them. However, the story of the defeat of the Armada was soon being widely disseminated. A number of versions of a commemorative portrait of Elizabeth were produced in an unusual landscape format that allowed for the inclusion of depictions of the English attack and the Spanish ships foundering in the storms. Rather than Philip, it was the Protestants who could claim that divine providence was at work in the defeat of the Catholic fleet: a Dutch medal struck in 1588 bore the inscription, *FLAVIT ET DISSIPATI SVNT* ('He blew and they were scattered').

The English were buoyant and keen to press on against the Spanish. Within a few months, a proposal was developed for Drake to command a

Counter-Armada, with Sir John Norris leading a land force. The fleet sailed from Plymouth on 18 April 1589 with more than 100 ships and over 20,000 officers and men. The intention was to destroy Spanish warships while they were being refitted and to send troops in support of Dom António, Prior of Crato and pretender to the Portuguese crown, which Philip II had held in a personal union with Spain since 1580. The English military intervention was reliant on the Portuguese rallying to support Dom António. If successful, it would have brought England huge sums of money and opened up new possibilities for plunder and trade in the overseas territories held by Portugal. However, there is a reason that the term 'Counter-Armada' is little recognised in England – it was a disaster. Drake ignored the instruction to attack the Spanish warships in the Bay of Biscay and instead acted in the belief that the Spanish had taken shelter in A Coruña. The English attacked but there was no military prize to seize, only determined resistance from the people of the town. The English moved on and Norris marched his troops overland to Lisbon. The march was poorly organised and the Portuguese showed little interest in supporting Dom António's claim. The fortress at Lisbon was too strong, and Norris left many of his sick and wounded behind to re-join Drake's ships. They tried to head for the Azores to attack the Spanish ships there, but, after coming under attack from a number of Spanish galleons, returned to Plymouth. Thousands of men had died, with comparable losses to those endured by the Spanish the previous year. Elizabeth quickly, and successfully, suppressed information about the expedition. In the English imagination, the defeat of the Spanish Armada stood in splendid isolation, a turning point in which the victory over the Spanish empire laid the foundations for England to realise its own imperial ambitions. To the Spanish, the attempted invasion of 1588 was merely one campaign in a lengthy war, offset by the English disaster the following year, and offering a model for further attacks in the 1590s that would take on the English in their first overseas colony: Ireland.

'Follow Me Upon Your Honour!': María Pita and the Siege of A Coruña

Monserrat Pis Marcos

Muller da soberana libertade,	*Woman of sovereign freedom*
os artilleiros danche alferezía	*the gunners grant you a lieutenancy*
e faite o mar patrona da cidade.	*and the sea makes you patron of the city.*
Din as miñas campanas, escoitade,	*My bells say, listen,*
de monte a monte e mais de ría a ría:	*from mountain to mountain and from inlet to inlet:*
O bronce meu, teu bronce foi María.	*my bronze was your bronze, María.*

'María das Batallas', Xesús Lorenzo Varela, 1944

It was May 1589. A woman stood on the rubble of a damaged city wall in north-western Spain, an English standard bearer dead at her feet, her lifeless husband nearby and a young daughter presumably not far away. Possibly in her late twenties or early thirties, her name was Mayor Fernández de la Cámara y Pita – though she would be known in the centuries to come as María Pita – and she had just 'fought with virility' against the English.

Born around 1556–62 in the port city of A Coruña, María Pita was the youngest daughter of two local shopkeepers. Little is known about her early years other than that she assisted her parents in the family business, located in the quarter of Pescadería. Between 1581 and 1585 María Pita was married to a butcher, Juan Alonso de Rois, with whom she had a daughter. Her second marriage, about two years later, to Gregorio de Rocamonde – also a butcher – was prematurely cut short by the English siege.

The prominent role of women in the defence of A Coruña against the Drake-Norris Expedition was highlighted by several contemporary sources, especially when the situation became very difficult for the besieged. In 1589 the city had a population of about 4,000 inhabitants and a garrison of 1,200 soldiers, so no hands could be spared to resist an army of over 27,000 men. Throughout the siege, women carried food supplies, water and stones, removed debris, loaded weapons, collected pewter to produce ammunition, buried the dead, kept spirits high, and were instrumental in strengthening the city's fortifications. María Pita, however, is one of only two named women among the many involved in these events. Her act of climbing atop a wall and killing an Englishman bearing a banner, a powerful symbol, while the besieged were desperately trying to prevent the attackers from entering the city, could not go unnoticed. In helping to turn the tables on the city's fate, she stepped into a heroic role usually reserved for men.

María Pita's life changed radically after 14 May 1589. A widow again, with a child to raise and living in a city in ruins, she quickly remarried, probably the year following the attack. Her third husband was a nobleman, Captain Sancho de Arratia, with whom she had one daughter, Francisca de Arratia. This third marriage was also short lived as Sancho de Arratia died in 1592, but it played a significant role in raising María Pita's social status. This ascent was further consolidated by her fourth marriage, in 1598 or 1599, to Gil de Figueroa, another nobleman who was squire at the Real Audiencia de Galicia. The two sons born from this union, Juan and Francisco Bermúdez de Figueroa, inherited their father's claim to nobility and had careers as a public servant and a soldier. María Pita was widowed one last time in 1613 and when she died, thirty years later, she left some property in Cambre and a modest estate in Ledoño.

Although no surviving accounts describe the personality of María Pita, her involvement in about thirty legal cases in the years after the siege and until her death in February 1643 paint quite a fierce and determined picture: in 1596 and 1606 she travelled to the royal court in Madrid to remind the king of her services in 'killing the General of the English' as well as in providing 'food, rope, bullets and all sorts of ammunition, and mattresses, and many other goods'. Both claims were resolved in her favour, and she obtained a lifetime military pension and the authorisation to trade in mules between Galicia and Portugal. Several of these judicial processes place María Pita as the recipient as well as the perpetrator of both verbal and physical abuse.

After her passing, María Pita's story was stripped of most biographical details to focus primarily on her participation in the siege. In 1662 the historian Felipe de Gándara y Ulloa dubbed her the 'Amazon of Galicia', and in 1726 the prominent Enlightenment scholar Fray Benito Jerónimo Feijoo described her as a 'Galician heroine'. Plays like *La Defensa de La Coruña por la heroica María Pita* (1784) by Antonio Valladares de Sotomayor and *María Pita o la heroína de Galicia* (1833) by Francisco Robello y Vasconi both lauded and romanticised María Pita, turning her into a legendary character whose name and actions epitomised the courageous resistance of the citizens of A Coruña at large, and of its women in particular. The second half of the nineteenth century witnessed her transition from hero to myth and from myth to symbol, in keeping with the Romantic spirit that buttressed contemporary nationalistic values through historical models that offered the allure of a glorious past mixed with a relatable socio-cultural specificity. In this process, however, the actual Mayor Fernández de la Cámara y Pita became a blurry shadow, her overpowering symbolism transcending and engulfing not only her own identity but the collective effort and struggles of many other unnamed women who withstood the siege alongside her. More recently, María Pita's eventful life and apparently fiery character have been reassessed and reinterpreted either as an isolated and unusual divergence from established gender roles and societal norms during Spain's Golden Age, or as a fascinating case study that evidenced that reality was a lot more nuanced in terms of social mobility and women's agency.

And yet, although A Coruña's local festivities and the city hall square are named after her, despite there being a museum dedicated to her memory and a handful of namesake streets scattered around Spain, today María Pita is little known outside of Galicia. Regardless of whether she actually killed someone, whether she used a pike or a sword, and what she might have said to inflame others, the fact remains that her resistance and that of her fellow townsfolk prevented an army from seizing a city. This is no small feat. One cannot help but wonder if her actions would have been met with the same silence in the official dispatches to the crown or, more recently, in nationwide Spanish secondary school textbooks had she been a man. Perhaps this story would now be common knowledge had it happened across the Channel or had it benefitted the English, considering the success of the propaganda campaign launched after the disastrous outcome of the 1588 Spanish Armada, and the opportunity squandered by Spain to respond in similar propagandistic terms following the failure of the English Armada a year later. The historiographical processes that lead to the 'footnotisation' of people and events are sometimes as fascinating as the facts themselves.

When the Drake-Norris Expedition set sail to Lisbon on 18 May 1589, two weeks after the start of the siege, the loss of about 1,500 men played heavily on the dwindling morale of the fleet. On the other hand, A Coruña had seen 1,000 deaths and sustained significant material damage, but had also accidentally stumbled upon one of its future heroines. The mythologising of 'María das batallas' – María of the battles – had just begun.

Map of A Coruña
Unidentified artist, c.1589
Paper, 300 x 400mm
British Library Mss 48021B

This maps shows A Coruña and its surroundings in Galicia, north-west Spain. It was probably made in connection with the 1589 expedition to A Coruña.

María Pita (1565–1643)
Unidentified artist, undated
Oil on canvas, 740 x 510mm
Casa-Museo de María Pita

Identified as María Pita in 2001, this portrait was found in Valencia. She wears luxurious attire, indicating that this shows María Pita later in life, after changes in social status through marriage.

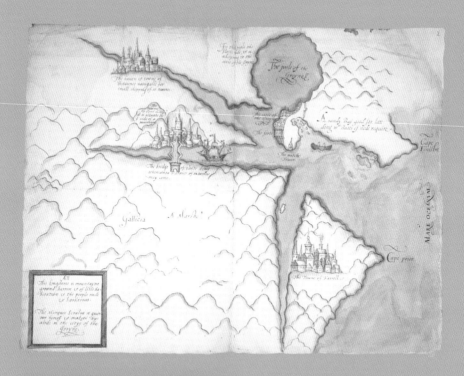

Empire

England's overseas empire began in Ireland. Following conquest by the Normans in the twelfth century, English monarchs had assumed lordship over Ireland, with the Lord Deputy acting on their behalf from Dublin Castle within the Pale. It was the Tudors who first attempted to impose centralised English control. Henry VIII was declared king of Ireland in 1541 after offering noble titles to a number of Gaelic lords to secure their support in the Irish parliament. However, increased oversight only served to demonstrate the fundamental incompatibility of Gaelic custom and English law, inflaming rebellion against the English and internal conflict between competing lords. By the time Elizabeth came to the throne, Ireland, which remained predominantly Catholic, was seen not only as a region to be controlled, but also as a potential threat to Protestant England. As a result, the English took increasingly forceful action, attempting to convince and coerce the Irish to accept the queen's rule; where that proved unsuccessful, they moved to colonise the country through the plantation of English settlers. To the patchwork power structures of lordships and old Anglo-Norman families were thus added the 'New English', the courtiers, soldiers and councillors of Elizabethan England who sought to make their names, and their fortunes, in Ireland. For many of these men, their experience in Ireland would inspire and inform their plans to expand England's empire further, looking to colonise lands further west, across the Atlantic in the Americas.

Queen Elizabeth I (1533–1603)
Marcus Gheeraerts the Younger, c.1592
Oil on canvas, 2413 x 1524mm
NPG 2561

This is likely one of the portraits that participants encountered in a grove during the entertainments staged by Sir Henry Lee at Ditchley. The secrets that the viewers were encouraged to decode included a number of Latin inscriptions and a sonnet, the jewelled armillary sphere worn by the queen, and the stormy sky on which she turns her back.

Walter Devereux, 1st Earl of Essex (1539–76)
Unidentified artist, inscribed 1572
Oil on panel, 1089 x 790mm
NPG 4984

This portrait commemorates Devereux's
investiture in the Order of the Garter in 1572
and his creation as earl of Essex that same year.
The inscription can be translated as 'Envy is the
companion of excellence'.

Sir Henry Sidney (1529–86)
George Gower, 1573
Oil on panel, 676 x 525mm
NPG 1092

This portrait was produced following Sidney's
recall from his first term as Lord Deputy. Writing
that he 'cursed, hated, and detested' the country,
he nonetheless campaigned for his reinstatement
with a programme of reform and returned to
Ireland in 1575.

The Elizabethan attempt to establish English authority in Ireland was led for long periods by Sir Henry Sidney. Appointed Lord Deputy in 1565, he mounted a campaign against the powerful Ulster chieftain Shane O'Neill and attempted to win supporters by brokering peace in the private war that had broken out between the earls of Ormond and Desmond. He also introduced a legislative programme to undermine the power of clan chieftains by removing their ability to levy money or service from their dependants. In these endeavours, he had support from English soldiers who had authority to impose martial law in order to suppress resistance. Thus, Sidney's attempted anglicisation of Ireland by statute and conciliation was enforced by the ruthlessness of his soldiers. One such soldier was Humphrey Gilbert, described as 'the most feared man in Ireland'. Gilbert was reported to have lined the pathway to his campaign tent with the heads of those he defeated in battle to terrorise their families when they came to treat for peace; Sidney knighted him for his service. However, despite wielding military and judicial power, Sidney was only able to pass part of his programme into law through the Irish parliament. Both the Old English and Gaelic communities were becoming increasingly wary of the English government and their distrust was only heightened by Sidney's support of plantation schemes.

Chief among these schemes was a proposal by Walter Devereux, Earl of Essex, to colonise Ulster, which lay beyond Sidney's authority and which Essex hoped to rule as Lord Deputy. While the queen instructed Essex to avoid bloodshed where possible, it soon became clear that his proposal to gain control by setting the Irish lords against each other, and against the Scottish MacDonnell clan in Antrim, would not suffice, particularly as disease and poor supplies weakened the English forces with each passing day. As costs spiralled and Essex petitioned for funding to establish permanent forts, Elizabeth and her councillors lost interest in the venture, preoccupied with the threat posed by Mary, Queen of Scots. Increasingly desperate, Essex turned to alternative methods to subdue the Irish lords. In 1574, he invited Sir Brian McPhelim O'Neill, ruler of Clandeboye,

Robert Devereux, 2nd Earl of Essex (1565–1601)
Marcus Gheeraerts the Younger, *c.*1597
Oil on canvas, 2180 x 1272mm
NPG 4985

Elizabeth I's last favourite, Robert Devereux was described as having 'a nature not to be ruled'. This portrait, in which he wears the robes of the Order of the Garter, was painted shortly after he led a raid on the Spanish city of Cádiz.

Henry Wriothesley, 3rd Earl of Southampton (1573–1624)
Robert Peake the Elder, *c.*1600
Oil on canvas, 2045 x 1219mm
NPG L114

Southampton was among Robert Devereux's most loyal companions. He supported Essex's attempt to regain influence at court by force and was found guilty of treason in 1601. Unlike Essex, he was spared execution. Southampton went on to be an active investor in England's overseas enterprises in the seventeenth century, equipping an expedition to Virginia in 1605.

to celebrate Christmas with him in Belfast; in the midst of the banquet, Essex's men slaughtered the company, apart from Sir Brian, his wife and his brother, who were sent to Dublin and executed. Soon after, Essex attempted to drive the Scots from Ulster, sending John Norris and Francis Drake to lead an expedition against Sorley Boy MacDonnell. On Rathlin Island, where MacDonnell had sent his family and those of his chief followers for safety, the English massacred hundreds. This did nothing to secure Essex's position in Ulster and he soon retreated to England, receiving a letter of comfort from the queen:

> You may think it has been a dear conquest to you, in respect of the great care of mind, toil of body, and intolerable charges you have sustained to the consumption of some good portion of your patrimony, but you have invested yourself with immortal renown.

Essex's 'immortal renown' secured him the title Earl Marshal of Ireland, but he did not enjoy it long, dying of dysentery in Dublin aged only 35 and leaving a young son, Robert, to inherit his title. Where Walter Devereux had viewed Ireland as a space in which to mount offensive campaigns, for Robert, England's defence would be the primary objective. He would not die there, but like so many of the English who attempted to subdue the country, his service in Ireland tarnished his reputation. By the 1590s Devereux was Elizabeth I's favourite, a martial hero who had symbolically assumed the role of the champion of international Protestantism after Philip Sidney bequeathed him his sword from his deathbed. His greatest triumph was a raid on Cádiz in 1596, although this primarily served to harden Philip II's resolve to invade England; Armadas departed Spain in 1598 and 1599, but were turned back by storms. The first of these proposed landing in Ireland before invading England, intending to rally Catholic support as the English had supported Protestants in the Spanish Netherlands. An earlier force consisting of Spanish and Italian volunteers funded by the pope and Philip II had already attempted this in support of the Desmond Rebellion in Munster in 1580. The shock that English fears of a Spanish attack in Ireland had been realised at Smerwick perhaps underpinned the Lord Deputy's order that the entire company should be executed after their surrender, an order that was reported to have been diligently carried out over two days under the supervision of a young captain from Devon, Humphrey Gilbert's half-brother Walter Ralegh.

The outbreak of rebellion across Ireland in 1593, led by Hugh O'Neill, Earl of Tyrone, was therefore not simply a threat to English authority in the region, but also raised the prospect of a new front in the war with Spain. After the English forces were routed at the Battle of the Yellow Ford in August 1598, it was feared that all of Ireland could be lost. Essex was commanded to impose order, crossing the Irish Sea at the head of the largest Tudor army ever to leave England. He was accompanied by Henry Wriothesley, Earl of Southampton, whom he had tried to appoint General of the Horse but who instead served as his personal attendant after the queen insisted the title be reversed; Southampton was out of favour after marrying one of her ladies-in-waiting without her permission. Essex hoped to move swiftly to crush Tyrone's forces in Ulster but he became bogged down in a war of attrition in Leinster and Munster, losing the queen's support as once again the costs of a campaign in Ireland spiralled out of control. Outnumbered and unsupported, Essex agreed to a truce with Tyrone and dispersed his army; Elizabeth was furious and Essex was imprisoned after racing back to London to seek the queen's forgiveness.

Sir Walter Ralegh (1554–1618)
Nicholas Hilliard, c.1585
Watercolour on vellum, 48 x 41mm
NPG 4106

This is thought to be the earliest portrait of Ralegh, painted by his fellow West Countryman, Nicholas Hilliard, around the time that Ralegh received his patent to colonise America.

131

Sir Humphrey Gilbert (1539?–1583)
Robert Boissard, c.1590–1603
Engraving, 184 x 126mm
NPG D20541

Gilbert's motto *Quid non* ('Why not') is perhaps
characteristically blunt. This engraving was
produced as part of a series of portraits of English
maritime adventurers.

Thomas Cavendish (1560–92)
Jodocus Hondius, c.1590
Engraving, 105 x 80mm
NPG 6677

A skilled navigator, Cavendish led the second
English circumnavigation voyage between 1585
and 1588. He died at sea in 1592 on a voyage to
open new trade routes with the Philippines, China
and Japan.

The English would ultimately triumph over O'Neill, gaining complete control over Ireland in 1603. Nine years of war nearly bankrupted the crown at a cost of over two million pounds, with thousands dying on the battlefields and during the famine caused by the English forces' scorched earth strategy. However, the costs of colonisation in Ireland did not temper English enthusiasm for it, and many looked across the Atlantic at the opportunities that might lie in creating settlements in the Americas. Two pioneers in this endeavour were Humphrey Gilbert and Walter Ralegh. Gilbert had returned from Ireland with a proposal to 'annoy the King of Spayne' through the destruction of Spanish fleets in Newfoundland and the establishment of an English colony in the West Indies to raid Spanish shipping. In 1578 he was given letters patent, granting him six years to search out 'remote heathen and barbarous landes' that could be held and governed by Gilbert and his heirs in perpetuity; the only restriction was that the land had not already been claimed by a Christian ruler. Gilbert was aware that he would need subjects, and proposed that the new colonies might offer both a solution to perceived overpopulation within the realm, and a suitable place for English Catholics to make a life beyond the jurisdiction of England's increasingly harsh recusancy laws. Departing from Plymouth in 1583, Gilbert first landed in Newfoundland, claiming the harbour of St John's and all land within two hundred leagues radius in Elizabeth's name. Gilbert's personal empire was short-lived; his ship, the *Squirrel*, went down in a storm off the Azores on his return journey to England. However, his approach to colonisation through royal charter would inspire his half-brother Walter to mount the first sustained campaign to establish English colonies in North America on behalf of the crown.

Walter Ralegh was a rising star at Elizabeth's court. An outsider from Devon, he seems to have secured his entry to the queen's innermost circle through the opportunistic discovery of valuable information among the letters of the soldiers massacred at Smerwick. He quickly became a model courtier, rivalling the aristocratic Robert Devereux through the performance of his intimacy with the queen through poetry. The queen generously rewarded her new favourite. In 1586, Ralegh was granted both the Derbyshire properties of Elizabeth's would-be assassin Anthony Babington, and 42,000 acres of land in the newly established Munster plantation, where land seized by the crown following the Desmond Rebellion was colonised through English settlement. However, Ralegh was already looking beyond Ireland, having secured a patent modelled on Gilbert's to seed colonies in North America. He first organised an expedition led by his cousin Sir Richard Grenville to set up a base for privateering on Roanoke Island, and then a fleet under John White to set up a farming settlement. However, war with Spain prevented relief voyages with supplies and both projects failed. In 1595, Ralegh looked even further afield to the north coast of South America, leading an expedition with dreams of discovering the lost golden city 'El Dorado' in Guiana. He returned without treasure but with stories of 'a country that hath yet her maidenhead, never sacked, turned, nor wrought', which he published in *The Discoverie of the Large, Rich and Bewtiful Empire of Guiana* (1596).

The tales of Tudor soldiers, sailors and explorers were to prove their most influential colonial legacy. Few could match Ralegh's prose, but the stories of their journeys circulated widely, providing inspiration and instruction to those who wished to follow them. Many were gathered together in Richard Hakluyt's *The Principall Navigations, Voiages, Traffiques and Discoueries of the English Nation*. First published in 1589 and then expanded in 1598, the compendium recorded English voyages across the world, including the circumnavigations of Francis Drake and Thomas Cavendish. Demonstrating a mind-set that would continue for centuries, the volume closely associated overseas enterprise with national pride, with the dedicatory epistle to Sir Francis Walsingham asserting that the English 'in compassing the vast globe of the earth more than once, have excelled all the nations and people of the earth'. England's would-be poet laureate Michael Drayton praised Hakluyt for creating a work that would 'enflame men to seek fame' in his ode 'To the Virginian Voyage', which concluded:

Michael Drayton (1563–1631)
Unidentified artist, 1599
Oil on panel, 597 x 457mm
NPG 776

Drayton is shown wearing a wreath of laurel leaves,
a symbol associated with poets. After the death of
Edmund Spenser in 1599, Drayton hoped to assume
the unofficial role of poet laureate.

You brave Heroique Minds,
Worthy your countries name,
That honour still pursuie,
Goe, and subdue,
Whilst loyt'ring Hinds
Lurke here at home, with shame.

It was in this environment that one of the most famous surviving Elizabethan works of art was produced, the so-called 'Ditchley' portrait of the queen. Painted as part of an elaborate entertainment staged by Sir Henry Lee in September 1592, the portrait is a rare surviving example in which information about the commissioner and the circumstances of the commission survive. However, beyond its original function within the entertainment, the composition speaks eloquently of the imperial ambitions that permeated English culture during the last years of Elizabeth's reign. Elizabeth looms over her country, shown as a queen whose authority naturally surpasses the constricting borders of her realm. It was through her royal blood as descendant of the Welsh Prince Madog ab Owain Gwynedd that the early colonisers laid claim to lands in the New World, reviving a legend of the plantation of Welsh colonies in North America in the twelfth century. As with portraits of the English circumnavigators, Francis Drake and Thomas Cavendish, the map on which Elizabeth stands, and the curve of the horizon line behind her, evoke both the practical value of maps in enabling England's expeditions and their political function as signifiers of the expanding boundaries of English authority. Earlier that year, Emery Molyneux had presented Elizabeth with the first terrestrial globe to be made in England. In addition, the lavish silks and jewels in which the queen is attired, and the ships plying the waters at her feet, demonstrate the fruits of the long-distance trading routes that the English wished to dominate. Only two weeks before the performance at Ditchley, the largest prize ever taken by English privateers – the

Portuguese carrack *Madre de Dios* ('Mother of God') – had sailed into Dartmouth, laden with pearls, diamonds, rubies, spices, gold and silk from the East Indies. The treasure would galvanise England's merchant adventurers to challenge the Spanish and Portuguese monopolies in trade with the Far East, sending out their own ships and seeking a royal charter to found the East India Company.

Terrestrial Globe
Emery Molyneux and Jodocus Hondius, 1603
Paper, plaster, ink, pigment and sand
Middle Temple Library

Molyneux was a mathematician and maker of mathematical instruments. This is a revised version of his globe, which was first presented to the queen at Greenwich in July 1592. The maps were engraved by Jodocus Hondius and chart the circumnavigations of both Francis Drake and Thomas Cavendish.

Fighting for Survival: Gráinne O Malley

Gillian Kenny

A most famous, feminine sea captain ... famous for her stoutness of courage ... commanding three galleys and 200 fighting men ... This was a most notorious woman in all the coasts of Ireland.
> Sir Henry Sidney's description of Gráinne in 1577

Gaelic pirate queen, female warlord, rebel, collaborator, mother, wife and, perhaps above all, consummate political operator, Gráinne O Malley (often anglicised as Grace O'Malley) was a woman of unique talent and achievements. She led her fleet of attack ships along the west coast of Ireland in the sixteenth century as her father did before her. She was a chieftain in all but name.

She was born in the 1530s into an Ireland that was about to undergo rapid and violent change as the Tudor monarchy began to enforce its aggressive anglicising agenda. Tudor administrators saw what they viewed as the politically disordered state of Ireland both as an opportunity – to close a backdoor for England's enemies – and as a means to gain large rewards for themselves in the form of a massive land grab. It was a dangerous and toxic combination, and ultimately resulted in the comprehensive dismantling and death of Gaelic Irish political, legal, social and cultural frameworks, as well as the establishment of divisions based on religion and culture which have affected Irish history for centuries since. The Tudor use of an annihilationist policy against Gaelic culture resulted in an 'age of atrocity' – endless warfare and genocidal acts of violence. Gráinne's is a story not only of high achievement but also extreme loss.

Her father was Owen Dubhdara (Black Oak) O Malley, lord of the Owles on the storm-battered west coast of County Mayo. Her first husband was Donal O Flaherty, a neighbouring chieftain. Her second was Richard an Iarainn (Iron Clad) Burke and they had a son, Theobald, who was reputedly born on one of his mother's ships while she was engaged in a battle. Sidney described Gráinne and Richard as follows: '[Gráinne] brought with her her husband, for she was aswell by sea as by land well more than Mrs Mate with him.' This remark alludes to her own power base, achieved independently of her husband: her fleet that prowled the sea lanes of western Ireland, imposing 'taxes' on passing ships and maintaining lucrative trading and fishing networks.

She was implicated in rebellions against English impositions in Mayo during the 1580s and 1590s, driven to action due to the oppressive activities of the English commander Richard Bingham and the need to buttress her son's claim to his father's lordship. After Theobald was arrested in 1593, a desperate Gráinne travelled to London to petition Elizabeth I, who ordered his release. In response, Gráinne offered the assistance of her own fleet of galleys to help the English forces in Mayo – a pragmatic way to ensure continuing English support. Gráinne's switch from rebel to supporter is indicative not only of the volatile situation in Ireland, but also of her commitment to securing the best deal possible for her and her family. She was an astute political operator.

After that, very little is heard of her again. It is not known exactly when she died but it was probably in the first decade of the seventeenth century. Depending on the author, she was either a fierce Irish rebel or a traitor to her own kind. In fact, she was neither of those, but rather a woman who was forced to make difficult political decisions to ensure her and her family's survival during a particularly dangerous period. That she succeeded in doing just that when so many others did not is testament to her skill.

The Kingdome of Irland from **The Theatre of the Empire of Great Britaine**
John Speed, 1616
British Library, MAPS C.7.C.19

Produced in 1616, this was an atlas designed to embed the idea of an emerging British Empire and its dominion over Ireland. Speed's depiction of the Irish as 'wilde' and barbaric reflected widely held views that served to justify their brutal treatment throughout the sixteenth century.

Sir Thomas Wyatt (1503?–1542)
After Hans Holbein the Younger, mid-sixteenth
century, based on a work of c.1540
Oil on panel, 470mm (diameter)
NPG 1035

This portrait relates to a woodcut attributed
to Holbein that was published in 1542 to
commemorate Wyatt's death; the pose draws on
the classical tradition of profile portraits on coins
and medallions.

Translation

The Tudors travelled widely. Many experienced other countries and cultures through diplomacy, war, exile, trade and colonisation, and the same currents brought people from across the world to England. At the same time, the proliferation of printing in the sixteenth century facilitated the broad dissemination of texts, allowing many more people to engage with information, ideas and fashions that originated far beyond England. In all these encounters, translation was key, serving both the practical function of enabling comprehension, and as the creative engine for the reshaping of ideas and language into a distinctive English form. Much of this activity took place within the court, a cosmopolitan space that enabled exchange between people whose education gave them the linguistic skills necessary to undertake translation. They were well aware that English was not an international language. If they wished to understand the world, they would have to translate it. The queen herself was perhaps the most famous linguist of the period, performing her fluency in a number of languages during audiences and in her correspondence. Elizabeth's skills were evident from a young age; aged 12, she presented her father with a prayer book that included a translation of Katherine Parr's *Prayers and Meditations* into Latin, French and Italian.

Elizabeth's choice of text reflected the priorities of the period, for the most important translations of the sixteenth century were religious. The establishment of Protestantism across Europe was underpinned by the translation of the Bible into the vernacular, allowing people to engage directly with the text in their own language. Where once unlicensed possession of English translations of the Scriptures had been punishable by death, the state now decreed that all churches should have a copy of the Bible in English. However, the establishment of the Church of England not only reshaped society, it made English the dominant language within the British Isles. This was enacted

Henry Howard, Earl of Surrey (1517?–1547)
After William Scrots, after 1566, based on a work
of 1546
Oil on panel, 480 x 301mm
NPG 4952

Although he was of noble birth, Surrey considered
Thomas Wyatt, who was a commoner, to be his
mentor in poetry; he published an extraordinary
elegy on Wyatt's virtues in 1542.

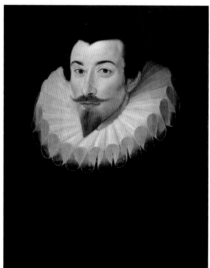

Sir John Harington (baptised 1560–1612)
Unidentified artist, c.1590–5
Oil on panel, 572 x 460mm
NPG 3121

Elizabeth I described Harington as 'that saucy poet,
my godson', and Harington embraced this identity.
In 1600 he sent a collection of epigrams to Lucy,
Countess of Bedford, that followed three psalm
paraphrases by Mary Sidney, describing his works
attending the paraphrases 'as a wanton page is
admitted to beare a torche to a chaste matrone'.

first by statute, with the 1549 Act of Uniformity enforcing the conduct of public worship in English, and then by assimilation, through regular exposure to English in the context of church services. In Cornwall, resistance to the new laws was ruthlessly suppressed during Edward VI's reign, heralding the decline of Cornish as a language. By contrast, Elizabeth ordered that all churches in Wales were required to hold Welsh translations of the Book of Common Prayer and the first full translation of the Bible into Welsh was published in 1588. This recognition of the Welsh language stood in contrast to Henry VIII's Laws in Wales Acts of 1535 and 1542, which stipulated that English should be the language of the law courts and of those holding public office. In prioritising religious conformity and its performance of loyalty to the state over linguistic uniformity, Elizabeth reduced the risk of rebellion. Nonetheless, these texts served to facilitate the anglicisation of Wales as the translated texts were intended to be consulted alongside the English versions. Elizabeth hoped that a similar approach might support the establishment of the Anglican faith in Ireland, commissioning an Irish translation of the New Testament in 1571.

While the translation of religious texts transformed society in the sixteenth century, the translation of poetry created new literary forms. When writing his influential handbook on poetry, *The Arte of English Poesie*, published in 1589, George Puttenham looked back to two men at Henry VIII's court as the 'first reformers of our English meter and stile': Thomas Wyatt and Henry Howard, Earl of Surrey. Wyatt, an ambassador who travelled widely in Europe, serving in France, at the papal court, and with Charles V, translated the sonnet form from Italian to English. Surrey, the son of the most powerful nobleman in England, the duke of Norfolk, invented English blank verse in his translation of Virgil's *Aeneid*. These two forms of poetry would provide the structure for the work of many of the most famous writers of England's literary renaissance in the late sixteenth century. One of the most ambitious works in blank verse from the period was itself a translation: John Harington's *Orlando Furioso in English Heroical Verse*. Ludovico

Ariosto's epic romance poem *Orlando Furioso* was first published in 1532; at nearly forty thousand lines, it is one of the longest poems in European literature. A later anecdote suggested that Harington, Elizabeth I's godson, was set to work at the queen's instruction, and banned from court until its completion, after sharing a lewd section of the poem among her ladies-in-waiting. It took Harington years; the translation was published, with a dedication to the queen, in 1591.

It is striking how many of the courtiers of Tudor England performed translation as a means of personal promotion in the guise of public service. Diplomacy took Thomas Chaloner across Europe over the course of his career in service to four Tudor monarchs. He travelled with Charles V to Innsbruck, Trent, Genoa and Lucca to join an expedition against the Ottomans in Algeria in 1541, delivered messages to Italian, Spanish and German mercenaries as clerk of the Privy Council during Edward VI's reign, negotiated with Mary of Guise in Scotland for Mary I, and served as Elizabeth's ambassador in Germany, Flanders and Spain. On his travels, Chaloner found the time to translate works by a wide-ranging selection of authors, including Ovid, Boethius and Ariosto; most importantly, he was the first English translator of Erasmus's *In Praise of Folly*, a satirical essay that the great Dutch humanist had written in London in 1509. One of Chaloner's literary friends was Thomas Sackville, another long-standing servant of the crown. Sackville would end his career as Lord High Treasurer, but his reputation as a writer was established in his youth when he co-authored *The Tragedie of Gorboduc* in 1561, which was the first English drama in blank verse. That same year, Sackville contributed a laudatory sonnet to Thomas Hoby's translation of a work that would reshape the very concept of the courtier: Baldassare Castiglione's *Il Cortegiano*. During the reigns of Henry VII and Henry VIII, the English court had modelled itself on the chivalric traditions of Burgundy and France, a legacy of cross-Channel dynastic alliances and the English claim to the French throne. However, with the revival of classical scholarship through Renaissance humanism, the English began to look to Italy for inspiration and

Sir Thomas Chaloner (1521–65)
Unidentified artist, 1559
Oil on panel, 711 x 546mm
NPG 2445

In his own time, Chaloner's most esteemed literary
productions were his Latin poems. In this portrait
the Latin inscription refers to Sardanapalus,
an exemplum of the vice of intemperance, and
Chaloner is shown in contemplation of the brevity
of human life, holding scales in which a blazing
book is weighted against the riches of the world.

**Thomas Sackville, 1st Earl of Dorset
(1536–1608)**
Unidentified artist, 1601
Oil on panel, 1105 x 876mm
NPG 4024

This portrait conceals an extraordinary act of
translation. It is painted over a depiction of the
Flagellation of Christ, derived from a fresco in
the Borgherini Chapel in Rome by Sebastiano del
Piombo after designs by Michelangelo Buonarotti.
It is possible that the artist failed to find a buyer for
the religious painting in England and so chose to
reuse the wooden panel.

Ralph Simons (active 1580–1610)
Unidentified artist, c.1595
Oil on panel, transferred from original panel,
567 x 430mm
NPG 7021

Simons holds a pair of dividers in his right hand
that would have taken the form of a dagger when
closed, echoing the weapons held by courtiers in
their portraits.

John Astley (c.1507–96)
Unidentified artist, 1555
Oil on canvas, 1700 x 875mm
NPG 6768

This portrait may have been produced during
Astley's journey to return to England from Italy in
1555; it is one of the earliest full-length portraits of
a non-royal English sitter.

models of behaviour. Castiglione's *Il Cortegiano* was first published in 1528 and its influence quickly spread across Europe; Thomas Cromwell, who had spent time in Italy in his youth, was among the first Englishmen to own a copy. Thomas Hoby's English translation offered a handbook of, in Sackville's words, 'what in Court a Courtier ought to be'.

However, translation did not only occur at court. It permeated all levels of society, both in the literal form of texts on diverse subjects that disseminated new knowledge, and in the broader sense in which ideas from other cultures were adopted by the English, often creating new professional opportunities. The concept of an architect was translated into England from Italy by John Shute, with the term first appearing in his 1563 publication *The First and Chief Groundes of Architecture*. By the 1590s, the English mason Ralph Simons was being styled as 'architecti sua aetate peritissimi' ('the most skilful architect of his time') on the frame that surrounded his portrait. In his retirement, Elizabeth's Master of the Jewel House, John Astley, published *The Art of Riding*. It was the first English treatise on horsemanship, and drew on both classical authors and the contemporary continental form of dressage that had first been codified by Federico Grisone in Italian. It built on a lifetime of experience; Astley had travelled in Italy during Mary I's reign and encouraged Thomas Blundeville's translation of Grisone's *Gli ordini di cavalcare* in 1560. Students were also involved in the circulation of new ideas through translation; the first treatise on painting published in English was a translation of Giovanni Paolo Lomazzo's 1585 *Trattato dell'arte della pittura, scultura et architettura* by the medical student Richard Haydock.

The centrality of translation to English culture was perhaps best expressed by the Anglo-Italian writer, lexicographer and translator John Florio at the end of Elizabeth's reign. In his address to the reader in his translation of the essays of the French philosopher Michel de Montaigne, he considered the question 'Shall I apologise translation?':

> What doe the best then, but gleane after others harvest? borrow their
> colors, inherite their possessions? What doe they but translate? Perhaps,
> usurpe? At least, collect? If with acknowledgement, it is well; if by stealth,
> it is too bad: in this, our conscience is our accuser; posteritie our judge.

Florio's critique of plagiarism was fair, not all translations were identified as
such. John Gerard, curator of the College of Physicians' physic garden and
superintendent of William Cecil's gardens, published the *Generall Historie of
Plants Gathered by John Gerarde of London*, commonly known as *The Herball*, in
1597. It would become one of the most widely owned books of the early 1600s,
but ultimately damaged Gerard's reputation, for his work was based on a near-
complete translation undertaken by Robert Priest of Rembert Dodoen's *Stirpium
historiae pemptades sex* (published in Antwerp in 1583), which Gerard had initially
been employed to edit.

Ultimately, translation would fuel the development of the English language
itself. The English interest in language in the sixteenth century is evident in
the number of primers and bilingual dictionaries that were produced. Where
diplomacy had always required at least Latin and French, now a courtier would
be expected to speak Italian as well, and likely Spanish, Dutch and German.
The English were also encountering far more languages through trade and
colonisation. Elizabeth I was presented with a Gaelic language primer in 1564
after expressing a desire to learn the language in order to treat with Shane
O'Neill when he visited the English court in 1562. Mark Ridley produced
a Russian–English dictionary while working as physician to the English
merchant community in Russia in the 1590s. Perhaps the most challenging act
of translation was undertaken by the scientist Thomas Harriot, who was tasked
by Walter Ralegh with learning the Carolina Algonquian language from Manteo
and Wanchese, two men who travelled to England from America on the return
of the first voyage to Roanoke. These new dictionaries not only allowed the

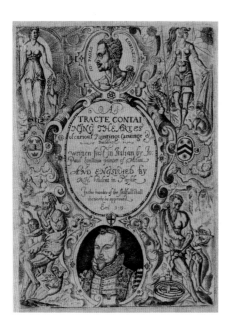

Richard Haydock (1569 or 1570–c.1642)
Possibly by Richard Haydock, published 1598
Engraving, 250 x 167mm
NPG D25462

Haydock had an amateur interest in the visual arts
and taught himself engraving. It is possible that
he engraved the frontispiece to his publication,
including his portrait at the base.

John Gerard (1545–1612)
William Rogers, published 1598
Engraving, 186 x 149mm
NPG D2756

Gerard is depicted holding some potato foliage in
this frontispiece to the *Herball*. The volume contains
the first full illustration of the plant; however, Gerard
confusingly transposed the potato into the context
of England's imperial ambitions by calling it the
'Virginian potato', even though it was known to have
originated in Peru.

English to comprehend other cultures, but also exposed the compilers to ideas and emotions that could not be adequately expressed in English. New words and phrases were needed. It was in this arena that John Florio made a transformative contribution. He had been born in London, the son of Italian Protestants who had sought sanctuary in England during Edward VI's reign, but had been forced into exile when Mary I restored Catholicism. On his return to England he found a role as a tutor to Henry Wriothesley, Earl of Southampton, and produced two Italian language primers, his *First Fruits* (1578) and *Second Fruits* (1591), and in 1598 *A World of Wordes*, an Italian–English dictionary. Though these books were ostensibly written in the service of teaching Italian to the English, they necessitated the creation of new words. Florio's contribution to the English language would come to stand third only to Chaucer and Shakespeare.

The role of translation in the transformation of English into an expressive, creative and adaptable language is embodied in the work of William Shakespeare. His grammar school education gave him Latin and the sources for many of his plays, ranging from Livy's histories and Cicero's speeches to the poetry of Virgil and Ovid. By the late sixteenth century he also had a wide range of contemporary texts upon which to draw. Blank verse and sonnets had become English modes of expression, and the vernacular stories of Europe were readily available in both their original languages and in translation. Harington's *Orlando Furioso* can be found in *Much Ado About Nothing*, Florio's Montaigne in *The Tempest*. The man whose writing would disseminate English history, language and culture across the world first encountered that world through translation.

William Shakespeare (1564–1616)
Martin Droeshout, 1632 or 1663–4
Engraving, 191 x 159mm
NPG 185

This posthumous portrait was produced for the
title page of the first complete publication of
Shakespeare's plays in 1623, known as the *First
Folio*. This version of the engraving dates from the
second or third editions of the plays in either 1632
or 1663–4.

The Literary Legacy of Mary Sidney, Countess of Pembroke

Catharine MacLeod

Mary Sidney was the most famous and influential female writer of her day, but 'Sidney's sister, Pembroke's mother' is how the poet William Browne referred to her in an epitaph – not an ideal summary of her life's achievements. He also calls her 'the subject of all verse' and tells us that she was 'fair and learn'd and good'. This reveals more about Elizabethan expectations of court women than it does about Sidney herself, although it does reflect the fact that what she achieved was done without breaking the boundaries of expected and approved female behaviour. The fact that she managed to live and work within relatively narrow social and cultural parameters and yet at the same time stretch them in ways that made a substantial literary contribution and inspired the women writers who came after her is a reflection of Mary Sidney's remarkable talent and character.

Mary Sidney was born in 1561, the daughter of Sir Henry Sidney and Lady Mary Dudley. She had three brothers – of whom one was Sir Philip Sidney, the poet – and three sisters. Her two older sisters both died young, and she was educated at home with her younger sister Ambrosia, learning French, Italian, Latin, possibly some Greek and Hebrew, the Scriptures and classical literature as well as needlework, lute playing and singing. When Ambrosia died in 1575, Mary was invited to court by Elizabeth I, where a marriage was soon arranged for her with Henry Herbert, Earl of Pembroke. She was 15; he had been widowed twice and was nearly 40 years old. In spite of the age gap, the marriage seems to have been successful, at least within the terms of the day. Four children are recorded as having been born, of whom three survived to adulthood. Pembroke's fabulous wealth and his country house, Wilton House in Wiltshire, facilitated Mary in both developing her own literary talents and supporting those of her family, dependants and contemporaries at court.

Her relationship to Philip Sidney was in fact key to Mary's evolution into a major literary figure. Philip Sidney spent time at Wilton, wrote and circulated poetry there and seems to have left several of his manuscripts in Mary's care. He dedicated his pastoral romance *Arcadia* (written and rewritten between 1578 and 1584) to her, indicating in the dedication that he had written it at her request and mostly in her presence. Wilton became, perhaps before Philip Sidney's death and certainly afterwards, a place where everyone seems to have been writing, including secretaries, Mary's children's tutor and the family physician. But ironically it was Philip's death that both stimulated and enabled his sister's public literary achievement. The year 1586 was a terrible one for her; first her father died in May, then her mother died in August, and finally Philip died in October, of wounds inflicted fighting Spain in the Battle of Zutphen. Mary retreated to Wilton for two years, but on her return to London in 1588, she began the work that would form her literary legacy.

A stream of poetic elegies had been written for Philip Sidney after his death, reflecting his popularity and the admiration in which he was held, as a man, soldier, courtier and writer, but also indicating the power of his uncle Robert Dudley, Earl of Leicester, whose patronage many of the poets had sought. After Dudley's death in 1588, Mary Sidney stepped into his shoes as the patron of Philip's admirers, and a new wave of elegies was written. Other important acts of literary patronage followed. In the meantime Mary was continuing with her own writing, and began to publish. She wrote her own elegies for Philip and a number of other elegiac poems; she also worked on highly influential translations. Translation was seen as an appropriate genre for women, but Mary was unusual in publishing her work and particularly in publishing under her own name.

Mary Sidney's most important works were her translation *Antonius* (1590, published 1592), from Robert Garnier's drama *Marc Antoine* (1578), and her metric paraphrases of the Psalms (completed by 1599). Philip Sidney had begun making verse translations of the Psalms, getting as far as Psalm 43. Mary Sidney completed his work and translated Psalms 44 to 150. Her sophisticated, poetic versions of the Psalms reveal her wide knowledge of Latin, French and other English editions, display a huge number of different verse forms and use various poetic devices to comment on contemporary politics and social experience. They were circulated widely during her lifetime, used in worship and some were set to music. *Antonius* was the first dramatisation of the story of Antony and Cleopatra in English, and one of the first English blank verse dramas. It inspired a fashion for plays primarily intended for private performance, and was an important influence on Shakespeare's *Antony and Cleopatra*.

The emphasis on originality that has dominated literary criticism since the Romantic period has tended to exclude translation from serious literary consideration. But, like many writers before and after her, Mary Sidney turned existing works into something new in her translations, enriching literary forms and the wider cultural context of her day, and creating a new template for women's creativity in early modern England.

**Mary Herbert, Countess of Pembroke
(1561–1621)**
Nicholas Hilliard, c.1590
Watercolour on vellum, 54mm (diameter)
NPG 5994

This miniature is typical of the portraits Hilliard
painted of women at Elizabeth's court in the 1580s,
at the height of his popularity. While the countess's
spectacular lace ruff and elaborately curled hair
reflect the time-consuming Elizabethan beauty
routine, the fresh flowers – including honeysuckle
and roses – pinned to her hair and bodice suggest
that she, like the flowers, is naturally beautiful.

TIMELINE

1485

Henry Tudor defeats Richard III at the Battle of Bosworth and founds the Tudor dynasty.

1511

The birth of Henry VIII and Katherine of Aragon's son is celebrated with a tournament at Westminster; John Blanke is among the court musicians who perform.

1526

Hans Holbein the Younger arrives in England with letters of introduction from the humanist scholar Desiderius Erasmus to potential patrons, including Thomas More.

1533

Thomas Cranmer marries Henry VIII and Anne Boleyn. The Act of Restraints in Appeals rejects papal authority in England, establishing the legal basis for the English Reformation.

1535

Thomas More and John Fisher are executed for their refusal to take the Oath of Supremacy. From Rome, Reginald Pole writes *Pro ecclesiasticae unitatis defensione (Defence of the Unity of the Church)*, opposing Henry VIII's spiritual authority.

1537

Jane Seymour dies soon after giving birth to the future King Edward VI. The first complete translations of the Bible into English are published.

1540

Henry VIII and Anne of Cleves are married, and they soon divorce. Thomas Cromwell is executed at Tower Hill along with Walter Hungerford; Henry VIII marries Catherine Howard the same day.

1541

The Irish parliament declares Henry VIII king of Ireland.

1545

Katherine Parr's *Prayers and Meditations* is the first book to be published in English by a woman under her own name.

1549

Rebellion rises in the west of England against the enforced use of Thomas Cranmer's *Book of Common Prayer*.

1550

The Stranger Church is established in London for émigré Protestant congregations.

1554

Parliament passes The Queen Regent's Prerogative Act and Mary I marries Philip II of Spain.

1556

Thomas Cranmer is burned at the stake in Oxford after watching Bishops Hugh Latimer and Nicholas Ridley suffer the same fate five months earlier.

1558

After being drawn into Spain's war with France, England loses Calais. John Knox publishes *The First Blast of the Trumpet Against the Monstrous Regiment of Women*. Elizabeth I appoints William Cecil Secretary of State on the first day of her reign.

1560

Catherine de' Medici is appointed Queen Regent of France for the first time.

1561

Publication of Thomas Hoby's *The Book of the Courtier*, translated from Baldassare Castiglione's *Il Cortegiano*.

1562

John Hawkins sails from Plymouth on his first slaving voyage.

1563

John Foxe's *Actes and Monuments*, popularly known as 'Foxe's Book of Martyrs', is published.

1569

A rebellion rises in northern England in support of Mary, Queen of Scots' claim to the English throne.

1570

Pope Pius V issues a papal bull, *Regnans in excelsis*, excommunicating Elizabeth I.

1572

Protestants are massacred in Paris on St Bartholomew's Day; Francis Walsingham and Philip Sidney shelter at the English embassy. In the Caribbean, Francis Drake forms an alliance with the Cimarrons against the Spanish with the assistance of Diego and attacks Nombre de Dios.

1575

Walter Devereux orders John Norris and Francis Drake to lead an attack on the MacDonnell clan on Rathlin Island.

1578

Humphrey Gilbert receives letters patent to colonise lands remote from England.

1581

Francis Drake returns to Plymouth following his three-year circumnavigation. Hercule-François, Duke of Alençon, visits the English court during negotiations to marry Elizabeth I.

1586

Robert Dudley accepts the role of Governor-General of the United Provinces; Philip Sidney dies following the Battle of Zutphen. Francis Walsingham exposes the involvement of Mary, Queen of Scots, in Anthony Babington's plot to assassinate Elizabeth I.

1588

Attack of the Spanish Armada. Bishop William Morgan's first complete translation of the Bible into Welsh is published.

1589

The English launch a Counter-Armada led by John Norris and Francis Drake. At A Coruña, they are beaten back by local citizens, including María Pita; the expedition is a failure.

1593

Gráinne O Malley sails to the court of Elizabeth I to petition for the release of her captured sons. William Shakespeare dedicates *Venus and Adonis* to Henry Wriothesley, Earl of Southampton.

1595

Walter Ralegh sails for Guiana in search of the riches of El Dorado.

1599

Mary Sidney finishes translating the Psalms into English, a project begun by her brother Philip Sidney before his death in 1586.

1600

The East India Company is founded by royal charter with a monopoly on English trade in Asia and the Pacific.

1603

The Tudor dynasty comes to an end with the death of Elizabeth I. She is succeeded by James VI of Scotland and I of England, Mary, Queen of Scots' son.

FURTHER READING

Biographical Dictionaries

Oxford Dictionary of National Biography (Oxford, 2004): ODNB
E. Town, 'A Biographical Dictionary of London Painters,
1547–1625', *The Walpole Society*, Vol. 76 (2014)

Tudor Portraits

C. Bolland, *Tudor & Jacobean Portraits* (London, 2019)
C. Bolland and T. Cooper, *The Real Tudors: Kings and Queens
Rediscovered* (London, 2014)
T. Cooper, A. Burnstock, M. Howard and E. Town, eds, *Painting
in Britain 1500–1630: Production, Influences and Patronage*
(Oxford, 2015)
R. Strong, *Tudor & Jacobean Portraits* (London, 1969)

Introduction: The Tudors

A. Ailes and R. Tittler, 'Arms Painting and the Life of Sir Henry
Unton', *British Art Journal*, Vol. 20, No. 3 (2020)
P. Barber, 'An Atlas For a Young Prince', in R. Palmer and
M. Brown, eds, *Lambeth Palace Library: Treasures from the
Collection of the Archbishops of Canterbury* (London, 2010)
A. Boorde, *The Fyrst Booke of the Introduction of Knowledge*, ed.
F.J. Furnivall (London, 1870)
R. Brown, ed., *Calendar of State Papers and Manuscripts
Relating to English Affairs, Existing in the Archives and
Collections of Venice, and In Other Libraries of Northern Italy*,
Vol. 2: 1509–1519 (London, 1867)
M. Greengrass, 'Unton [Umpton], Sir Henry (c. 1558–1596)',
ODNB
R. Holinshed, *The Firste Volume of the Chronicles of England,
Scotlande and Ireland* (London, 1577)
M. de Montaigne, *The Essays or Morall, Politike and Militarie
Discourses of Lo: Michaell de Montaigne*, trans. J. Florio
(London, 1603)
M. Rudick, 'The Text of Ralegh's Lyric, "What Is Our Life"',
Studies in Philology, Vol. 83, No. 1 (1986)
R. Strong, 'Sir Henry Unton and his Portrait: An Elizabethan
Memorial Picture and its History', *Archaeologia*, Vol. 99 (1965)

A New Dynasty/Insights into John Blanke's
Image from The John Blanke Project

S. Anglo, *The Great Tournament Roll of Westminster* (Oxford,
1968)
C.S.L. Davies and J. Edwards, 'Katherine [Catalina, Catherine,
Katherine of Aragon] (1485–1536)', *ODNB*
S. Foister, 'Holbein, Hans, the younger (1497/8–1543)', *ODNB*
S.J. Gunn, 'Henry VII (1457–1509)', *ODNB*
R. Horrox, 'Elizabeth [Elizabeth of York] (1466–1503)', *ODNB*

E.W. Ives, 'Henry VIII (1491–1547)', *ODNB*
M.K. Jones and M.G. Underwood, 'Beaufort, Margaret [known
as Lady Margaret Beaufort], countess of Richmond and Derby
(1443–1509)', *ODNB*
M. Kaufmann, 'Blanke, John (fl. 1507–1512)', *ODNB*
M. Kaufmann, *Black Tudors: The Untold Story*
(London, 2017)
O. Nubia, *Blackamoores: Africans in Tudor England*
(London, 2013)
The John Blanke Project Historians: https://www.johnblanke.
com/historians.html

The King's Court/Walter Hungerford and the 1533
Buggery Act

C. Arnold, *City of Sin: London and its Vices* (London, 2010)
D.J. Ashton, 'Hungerford, Walter, Baron Hungerford of
Heytesbury (1503–1540)', *ODNB*
S. Baker House, 'More, Sir Thomas [St Thomas More]
(1478–1535)', *ODNB*
X. Brooke and D. Crombie, *Henry VIII Revealed: Holbein's
Portrait and its Legacy* (London, 2003)
L. Crompton, *Homosexuality and Civilization*
(Cambridge, 2003)
J. Gairdner and R.H. Brodie, eds, *Letters and Papers,
Foreign and Domestic, of the Reign of Henry VIII*,
Vols 9: *August–December 1535*; 10: *January–June 1536*;
15: *1540*; XVIII: *Part 1 January–July 1543* (London, 1886–1901)
R. Hutchinson, *Henry VIII: The Decline and Fall of a Tyrant*
(London, 2019)
M. Kirby, 'The Sodomy Offence: England's Least Lovely
Criminal Law Export?' in C. Lennox and M. Waites, eds,
*Human Rights, Sexual Orientation and Gender Identity in
The Commonwealth* (London, 2013)
H. Leithead, 'Cromwell, Thomas, earl of Essex (b. in or before
1485, d.1540)', *ODNB*
C.H. Miller, L. Bradner and C.A. Lynch, *The Yale Edition
of The Complete Works of St Thomas More* (New Haven and
London, 1974)
J.G. Nichols, *Literary Remains of King Edward the Sixth*
(London, 1857)
G. Oestmann, 'Kratzer, Nicolaus (b.1486/7, d. after
1550)', *ODNB*
K.M. Phillips and B. Reay, *Sex Before Sexuality: A
Premodern History* (Cambridge, 2011)
R. Rex, 'Fisher, John [St John Fisher] (c.1469–1535)', *ODNB*
J.J. Scarisbrick, 'Warham, William (1450?–1532)', *ODNB*
K. Van Mander, *The Lives of the Illustrious Netherlandish
and German Painters, From the First Edition of the
Schilderboeck 1604*, ed. Hessel Miedema, Vol. 1: *The
Text* (Doornspijk, 1994)

The Reformation in England/Reginald Pole, Catholic Reform and Religious Reconciliation

E. Duffy, *Fires of Faith: Catholic England under Mary Tudor* (New Haven and London, 2009)
J. Edwards, *Archbishop Pole* (Farnham, 2014)
D. Fenlon, *Heresy and Obedience in Tridentine Italy: Cardinal Pole and the Counter-Reformation* (Cambridge, 1972)
M. Firpo, 'The Italian Reformation', in R.P. Hsia, ed., *A Companion to the Reformation World* (Oxford, 2004)
D. Hoak, 'Edward VI (1537–1553)', *ODNB*
D. MacCulloch, 'Cranmer, Thomas (1489–1556)', *ODNB*
T.F. Mayer, *Reginald Pole: Prince & Prophet* (Cambridge, 2000)

Queenship/'We Princes Who Be Women': Catherine de' Medici in France

S. Adams, 'Dudley, Robert, earl of Leicester (1532/3–1588)', *ODNB*
B.L. Beer, 'Jane [née Jane Seymour] (1508/9–1537)', *ODNB*
P. Collinson, 'Elizabeth I (1533–1603)', *ODNB*
S. Doran, 'Elizabeth I and Catherine de' Medici', in G. Richardson, ed., '*The Contending Kingdoms': France and England 1420–1700* (London, 2008)
E.W. Ives, 'Anne [Anne Boleyn] (c.1500–1536)', *ODNB*
S.E. James, 'Katherine [Kateryn, Catherine] [née Katherine Parr] (1512–1548)', *ODNB*
C. Jordan, 'Woman's Rule in Sixteenth-Century British Political Thought', *Renaissance Quarterly*, Vol. 40, No. 3 (1987)
G. Lebel, 'British-French Artistic Relations in the XVI century', *Gazette des Beaux-Arts*, Vol. 33 (1948)
A. Plowden, 'Grey [married name Dudley], Lady Jane (1537–1554)', *ODNB*
G. Redworth, 'Philip [Philip of Spain, Felipe] (1527–1598)', *ODNB*
A. Weikel, 'Mary I (1516–1558)', *ODNB*

Holding the Throne/Anthony Babington and the Memorialisation of a Conspiracy

S. Adams, 'Dudley, Robert, earl of Leicester (1532/3–1588)', *ODNB*
S. Adams, A. Bryson and M. Leimon, 'Walsingham, Sir Francis (c.1532–1590)', *ODNB*
S. Doran, ed., *Elizabeth and Mary: Royal Cousins, Rival Queens* (London, 2021)
E. Goldring, 'Talbot, George, sixth earl of Shrewsbury (c.1522–1590)', *ODNB*
J. Goodare, 'Mary [Mary Stewart] (1542–1587)', *ODNB*
W.T. MacCaffrey, 'Cecil, William, first Baron Burghley (1520/21–1598)', *ODNB*
M. Peltonen, 'Bacon, Francis, Viscount St Alban (1561–1626)', *ODNB*
R. Shephard, 'Sidney, Robert, first earl of Leicester (1563–1626)', *ODNB*

E. Town and J. David, 'Daniël van den Queborn, Painter to the House of Orange and its English Allies in the Netherlands', in L. Wrapson, V. Sutcliffe, S. Woodcock and S. Bucklow, eds, *Migrants: Art, Artists, Materials and Ideas Crossing Borders* (Cambridge, 2019)
P. Williams, 'Babington, Anthony (1561–1586)', *ODNB*
H.R. Woudhuysen, 'Sidney, Sir Philip (1554–1586)', *ODNB*
N. Younger, 'Robert Peake (c.1551–1619) and the Babington Plot', *British Art Journal*, Vol. 14, No. 2 (2013)

Piracy, Privateering and Trade/Diego, Drake and Piracy in Panama

J.D. Alsop, 'Strangeways, Henry (d. 1562)', *ODNB*
K. Andrews, *Drake's Voyages* (London, 1967)
J.P. Collier, ed., *Old Ballads, From Early Printed Copies of the Utmost Rarity* (London, 1840)
S. Doran, ed., *Elizabeth and Mary: Royal Cousins, Rival Queens* (London, 2021)
M. Kaufmann, 'Diego (d.1579)', *ODNB*
H. Kelsey, 'Drake, Sir Francis (1540–1596)', *ODNB*
V. Klinkenborg and R. Kraemer, *The Drake Manuscript in the Pierpont Morgan Library: Histoire Naturelle des Indes* (London, 1996)
C. MacLeod, 'Flicke, Gerlach [Garlick, Garlicke] (d.1558)', *ODNB*
B. Morgan, 'Hawkins, Sir John (1532–1595)', *ODNB*
P. Nichols, *Sir Francis Drake Revived* (London, 1623)
C. Smith, *Black Africans in the British Imagination: English Narratives of the Early Atlantic World* (Baton Rouge, 2016)
D.J.B. Trim, 'Carleill, Christopher (1551?–1593)', *ODNB*
R. Tyler, ed., *Calendar of Letters, Despatches, and State Papers, Relating to the Negotiations between England and Spain, preserved in the archives at Vienna, Simancas, Besançon and Brussels*, Vol. 11: *Edward VI and Mary 1553* (London, 1916)

The Spanish and English Armadas/'Follow Me Upon Your Honour!': María Pita and the Siege of A Coruña

X. Cabaleiro, 'María Pita: A Xénese dun Mito', *Festa da Palabra Silenciada*, No. 7 (1990)
S. Doran, ed., *Elizabeth and Mary: Royal Cousins, Rival Queens* (London, 2021)
L. Gorrochategui Santos, *The English Armada: The Greatest Naval Disaster in English History* (London, 2018)
L.A. Knafla, 'Stanley, Henry, fourth earl of Derby (1531–1593), *ODNB*
A.M. Poska, *Women and Authority in Early Modern Spain: The Peasants of Galicia* (New York, 2005)
M. del Carmen Saavedra Vázquez, 'Guerra, Mujeres y Movilidad Social en la España Moderna: El Ejemplo de María Pita', in

Carmen Balboa López and Herminia Pernas Oroza, eds, *Entre nós. Estudios de Arte, Xeografía e Historia en Homenaxe ó Profesor Xosé Manuel Pose Antelo* (Santiago de Compostela, 2001)
M. del Carmen Saavedra Vázquez, *María Pita. Una Aproximación a su Vida y a su Tiempo* (A Coruña, 2003)
L. Seoane, *María Pita e tres retratos medievales* (Buenos Aires, 1944)

Empire/Fighting for Survival: Gráinne O Malley

M. Drayton, *Poems Lyrick and Pastorall* (London, 1606)
P.E. Hammer, 'Devereux, Robert, second earl of Essex (1565–1601)', *ODNB*
P. J. Duffy, D. Edwards and E. FitzPatrick, eds, *Gaelic Ireland, c.1250–c.1650: Land, Lordship and Settlement* (Dublin, 2001)
D. Edwards, P. Lenihan and C. Tait, eds, *Age of Atrocity: Violence and Political Conflict in Early Modern Ireland* (Dublin, 2007)
A. Gallay, *Walter Ralegh: Architect of Empire* (New York, 2019)
P. Honan, 'Wriothesley, Henry, third earl of Southampton (1573–1624)', *ODNB*
C. Lennon, *Sixteenth-Century Ireland: The Incomplete Conquest* (Dublin, 1994)
W.T. MacCaffrey, 'Sidney, Sir Henry (1529–1586)', *ODNB*
M. MacCurtain and M. O'Dowd, eds, *Women in Early Modern Ireland* (Edinburgh, 1991)
S.M. Maxwell, 'Cavendish, Thomas (*bap.* 1560, *d.*1592)', *ODNB*
J.J.N. McGurk, 'Devereux, Walter, first earl of Essex (1539–1576)', *ODNB*
M. Nicholls and P. Williams, 'Ralegh, Sir Walter (1554–1618)', *ODNB*
M. O'Dowd, 'O'Malley, Gráinne [Grace] (*fl.* 1577 1597)', *ODNB*
A.L. Prescott, 'Drayton, Michael (1563–1631)', *ODNB*
R. Rapple, 'Gilbert, Sir Humphrey (1537–1583)', *ODNB*

Translation/The Literary Legacy of Mary Sidney, Countess of Pembroke

S. Bakewell, 'Haydock, Richard (1569/70–c.1642)', *ODNB*
S. Brigden, 'Howard, Henry, earl of Surrey (1516/17–1547)', *ODNB*
C. Burrow, 'Wyatt, Sir Thomas (*c.*1503–1542)', *ODNB*
T. Cooper, *Citizen Portrait: Portrait Painting and the Urban Elite of Tudor and Jacobean England and Wales* (New Haven, 2012)
M.P. Hannay, 'Herbert [*née* Sidney], Mary, countess of Pembroke (1561–1621)', *ODNB*
M.P. Hannay, N.K. Kinnamon and M.G. Brennan, eds, *The Collected Works of Mary Sidney Herbert, Countess of Pembroke* (Oxford, 1998)
T. Hoby, *The Courtier of Count Baldessar Castilo Divided into Four Books* (London, 1561)
P. Holland, 'Shakespeare, William (1564–1616)', *ODNB*
C. Merton, 'Astley, John (*c.*1507–1596)', *ODNB*
M. de Montaigne, *The Essays or Morall, Politike and Militarie Discourses of Lo: Michaell de Montaigne*, trans. J. Florio (London, 1603)
C.H. Miller, 'Chaloner, Sir Thomas, the elder (1521–1565)', *ODNB*
D. O'Connor, 'Florio, John (1553–1625), *ODNB*
G. Puttenham, *The Arte of English Poesie Contrived Into Three Books* (London, 1589)
J. Scott-Warren, J., 'Harington, Sir John (*bap.* 1560, *d.*1612)', *ODNB*
M. Smolenaars, 'Gerard, John (*c.*1545–1612)', *ODNB*
R. Zim, 'Sackville, Thomas, first Baron Buckhurst and first earl of Dorset (*c.*1536–1608)', *ODNB*

ELIZABETH   REGINA

THE HOLBURNE MUSEUM ACKNOWLEDGEMENTS

In addition to those already acknowledged, I would like to extend my thanks to those at the Holburne Museum who have made the Bath presentation of *The Tudors: Passion, Power and Politics* possible: Chris Stephens, Director, for inspiring and motivating; Sylvie Broussine, Assistant Curator, and Nina Harrison Leins, Exhibitions Coordinator, for their keen eye for detail, generosity and commitment; Emma Morris, Head of Business and Development, Katie Jenkins, Head of Communications, Louise Campion, Learning and Engagement Lead, and Olivia Mason, Development Manager, for their expertise and support. Thanks also to our Front of House team, volunteers and all those we work with externally.

Monserrat Pis Marcos
Curator, The Holburne Museum

NATIONAL MUSEUMS LIVERPOOL ACKNOWLEDGEMENTS

I would particularly like to thank Lucy Johnson, Head of Art Gallery Exhibitions, and Fiona Slattery Clark, Curator of Decorative Art, for their dedication to *The Tudors: Passion, Power and Politics* at the Walker Art Gallery. The exhibition would not have been possible without the commitment, expertise and support of a wide team of colleagues at National Museums Liverpool. We are extremely grateful to everyone for their contribution and extend our particular thanks to the project team. National Museums Liverpool would also like to thank our partners, the National Portrait Gallery and the Holburne Museum, and all of our lenders, for making this exhibition possible.

Kate O'Donoghue
Curator of International Fine Art,
National Museums Liverpool

NATIONAL PORTRAIT GALLERY ACKNOWLEDGEMENTS

The idea of staging a two-venue Tudor exhibition as a collaboration between the National Portrait Gallery, the Holburne Museum and National Museums Liverpool (Walker Art Gallery) first arose in 2019. Despite the unique challenges of the years 2020 and 2021, Chris Stephens, Director at the Holburne, and Sandra Penketh, Executive Director of Galleries and Collections Management, and Fiona Philpott, Director of Exhibitions, at National Museums Liverpool, worked alongside Sarah Tinsley, Executive Director Programmes & Partnerships at the Gallery, to ensure that the project could continue. We are incredibly grateful for the committed support from colleagues across departments at each of the partners that have made the publication of this book and the delivery of the exhibitions in Bath and Liverpool possible.

We would also like to extend our particular thanks to the contributors to this book, whose pieces inspired each of us in our own research and writing: Michael Ohajuru, Frederick E. Smith, Susan Doran, Cassander Smith, Gillian Kenny and Catharine MacLeod. Our thanks also to the National Portrait Gallery's publishing team for the book's production: Anna Starling, Director of Commercial; Kara Green, Publishing Manager; Tijana Todorinovic, Project Editor; Mark Lynch, Picture Library Manager; and Tom Love, Publishing Executive. We are also grateful to Alison Effeny for the proofreading of the catalogue, and to Joe Ewart for working on the wonderful design of this publication.

I would particularly like to thank the National Programmes Team, Laura Down, Head of National Programmes, and Sophie Farmer, National Programmes Assistant; the Collections team for their commitment to this project, including Edward Purvis, Head of Collections Services, and Richard Hallas, Senior Conservation Manager; and the conservators who have prepared the works for both exhibitions, Stuart Ager, Ffion Howels, Sally Higgs, Claire Irvine and Alice Powell. Thanks also go to Simon and Tom Bobak for their assessments of many of the panel paintings. The exhibitions would not have been possible without the expertise of the Loans and Art Handling teams, led by Clare Greenaway, Loans Registrar, and Karl Lydon, Art Handling Manager. I would also like to thank our Communications team, led by Denise Vogelsang, Director of Communications and Digital, with Laura McKechan, Senior Communications Manager, and Emily Summerscale, Marketing Manager, and the Gallery's Curatorial team, led by Alison Smith, Chief Curator.

Charlotte Bolland
Senior Curator, Research and 16th Century Collections, National Portrait Gallery

PICTURE CREDITS

Published in Great Britain
by National Portrait Gallery Publications
National Portrait Gallery
St Martin's Place
London WC2H 0HE

Published to accompany the exhibition:
The Tudors: Passion, Power and Politics
The Holburne Museum, Bath
28 January to 8 May 2022
Walker Art Gallery, National Museums Liverpool
21 May to 29 August 2022

This exhibition has been made possible as a
result of the Government Indemnity Scheme. The
National Portrait Gallery, London, would like to
thank HM Government for providing indemnity
and the Department for Digital, Culture, Media
and Sport and Arts Council England for
arranging indemnity.

Every purchase supports the National Portrait
Gallery, London. For a complete catalogue of
current publications, please visit our website at
www.npg.org/publications

ISBN 978 1 85514 598 6

A catalogue record for this book is available from
the British Library

10 9 8 7 6 5 4 3 2 1

Director of Commercial: Anna Starling
Publishing Manager: Kara Green
Project Editor: Tijana Todorinovic
Picture Library Manager: Mark Lynch
Publishing Executive: Tom Love
Design: Joe Ewart
Proofreader: Alison Effeny
Printed in Italy by Printer Trento
Reproductions by DL Imaging

Front cover: Queen Elizabeth I, unidentified artist,
*c.*1588, NPG 541 (detail)

Back cover: Sir Francis Drake, unidentified artist,
*c.*1581, NPG 4032 (detail)

FSC
www.fsc.org
MIX
Paper from
responsible sources
FSC® C015829